CONFESSIONS
OF AN ENGLISH
TEACHER

CONFESSIONS OF AN ENGLISH TEACHER

*How English Departments in
High Schools and Community Colleges
Can Improve Instruction*

RICHARD P. SINAY

To Sue Krenwinkle for Her Incredible Support

To Current and Future English Teachers

"Teaching is perhaps the most privatized of all the public professions. Though we teach in front of students, we always teach solo, out of collegial sight—in contrast to surgeons and lawyers who work in the presence of others who know their craft well. When we walk into our workplace, the classroom, we close the door on our colleagues. When we emerge, we rarely talk about what happened or what needs to happen next, for we have no shared experience to talk about."

The Courage to Teach: Exploring the Inner Landscape of a Teacher's Life
—Parker J. Pilmer

Contents

Preface

I wrote this book as a follow-up to my memoir *Confessions of an English Teacher: A Memoir of My Teaching Years*. I wanted to elaborate on the claims that I made in that book. I had taught at six high schools and seven community colleges, so I was qualified to speak about my experiences and the conclusions I drew from those experiences. My educational background includes finishing a B.A. and M.A. in English, an M.S. in Reading, a Reading Specialist Credential, a Standard Secondary Credential for Language Arts, an Administrative Services Credential, and a Community College Language Arts Credential. Besides the previous, I finished the coursework of thirty units for a master's in education with a specialization in administration. I also spent three years studying writing and teaching through extension courses at the University of California at Irvine, a college near my home in Irvine. Although I may make controversial statements about teaching English, the purpose is not to create controversy as much as it is to open the discussion about teaching English and the operation of an English department.

I was sitting in a department meeting when we were asked to break into groups during a think tank session. The principal approved time that we could use to encourage curriculum development and improvement. The principal attended the meeting and sat down with our group, and we began entertaining ideas about improving the English department's curriculum. I started a narrative by discussing how an English department should have a coordinated writing program. The writing program would ensure students were being prepared for writing at the college level. I suggested that the Modern Language Association Style books be used to effectively teach students how to document a paper on a controversial subject. The entire writing program would be designed for both levels of instruction: honors and college-bound students. After the meeting, the principal approached me and said I had discussed some great ideas and that he looked forward to more work. That was as far as the idea went. I advocated that the English department organize the writing for the four years student take an English class. I had already instituted the requirement that freshman to senior year write an MLA-style research paper. However, only some teachers required their students to do the paper.

This story illustrates that great ideas can go nowhere in an English department. Despite the praise of the principal, there needed to be a follow-up by the English department chair. This may be why English departments stay the same year after year, decade after decade. It seems impossible to break the traditions of an English department. Is it that English teachers are independent contractors who do not wish to be dictated what is taught to students? I know I have seen plenty of that behavior in my long career. Or is it that English teachers need to be more relaxed with all the reading they need to do for class preparation and all the papers they are responsible for grading? Everything I discuss in this book is about improving the operation of an English department. This book is a follow-up to my book *Confessions of an English Teacher: A Memoir of My Teaching Years*. I want to expand on the comments and ideas from that book and make recommendations for change in teaching English. I want to share those recommendations and expand upon the concepts introduced in the memoir.

It may be bold to make the claims I make in this book, but my experiences with various English departments at both the high school and community college levels give me enough credibility. I taught at six different high schools over a thirty-five-year career and learned a great deal about each department's approaches to teaching English. I also taught part-time at seven community colleges for twenty-eight years, And I drew conclusions from my experience. I could not write this without all those experiences, so I want to share those observations and recommendations with current and future English teachers.

Part I:
High School Recommendations

Introduction To High School Recommendations

In *Confessions of an English Teacher: A Memoir of My Teaching Years,* I drew several conclusions about teaching English at the high school level. As a follow-up to that book, I want to embellish those conclusions and address the teaching of writing, reading, and literature related to teaching English. I wish to make recommendations that will improve the teaching of English at the secondary level.

Part I will concern itself with the teaching of reading. A Title I reading program should exist for students reading two grade levels below the one they are in. If one is a junior reading at the 9th-grade level, a reading class is necessary to bring the student up to grade-level reading ability. Reading classes are essential for improving students' deficient language skills. It is recommended that the school and district apply for Title I reading support. The Title I program is designed explicitly for underprivileged students so they can increase their reading skills and comprehension skills. This requires the establishment of a reading lab, hiring a reading specialist, and school support for the program.

Part II will address the English department's hallmarks of teaching writing. The hallmarks necessary for a great English department are vital to success. Chapter five will discuss the need for an organized writing program. Chapter six will claim that teaching writing as a process is the most beneficial experience for a student writer. Chapter seven will discuss the need for a writing evaluation program. Chapter eight will argue that grammar should be taught in the context of writing and not outside of a writing project. Chapter nine will discuss the importance of teaching usage in the context of teaching writing. Furthermore, chapter ten will discuss the importance of preparing students for the writing done in college. Chapter eleven will discuss the need to teach the appropriate essays to college-bound students. Finally, the last chapter in this section will discuss the importance of a writing lab for developing the student's writing. These recommendations can be entirely rejected or embraced as good ideas for English departments to adopt or reject for whatever reasons. They are my suggestions from my thirty-five-year career as a high school teacher and twenty-eight part-time years as a college teacher. They are suggestions an English department can implement to strengthen its program.

Part III will address the use of literature in the secondary classroom. The literature and nonfiction taught to students should be carefully selected so they can read it. The literature and nonfiction choices should consider The ethnic composition of the students. Literature and nonfiction should be well organized to encourage student literacy growth. I also advocate a well-constructed vocabulary program designed for students reading literature. Additionally, I believe in a solid independent reading program.

Part IV of the high school recommendations will suggest several characteristics of an English department that all department members can appreciate. These English department hallmarks include behaviors a department can exercise to improve performance. Those behaviors include preparing course outlines and lesson plans for new teachers. The hallmarks also call for an established writing program and an effective assessment program. A great English department will also have an English department chair with leadership skills and a master's degree in English, reading, or composition. The English department will require a master's in English to teach any honors class or AP course. Also, the English department will use the best English teachers to mentor student teachers. More importantly, an English department that hires the best candidates for new jobs and a department that knows current research on teaching writing, reading, literature, and nonfiction.

My various high school experiences gave me a different perspective on how an English department operates, allowing me to draw different conclusions about its operation. Although I do not have all the answers, I guarantee the reader that I have some. Still, I present options for English departments to collaborate more to advance our students' literacy in this challenging world.

Part A:
Reading Hallmarks

Chapter 1:
Great English Departments Have a Title I Reading Program and a Reading Lab

The high school where I taught most of the years had no Title I program or reading lab. High Schools that qualify for Title I funding should apply for the money. The Placentia-Yorba Unified School district ignored applying for funding during my twenty-six years there. Title I funding is for those disadvantaged students coming to school reading two grade levels below their actual grade. Ninth-grade students from junior high school reading at the 7th-grade level at the beginning of the school year qualify for assistance in the Title I reading program. Establishing a Title I reading program and a reading lab is the mark of a Great English Department.

Applying for Title I reading program funding involves writing a grant and applying to the Federal government for financing. If the school qualifies, the funding will be sent to the district to hire a reading specialist to create a reading lab for disadvantaged students. As I have already written, the Fullerton Union High School District had a Title I reading program at Fullerton High School, Buena Park High School, and Troy High School.

Each had a reading lab where students could quietly read, listen to stories, and develop their vocabulary and comprehension skills. The goal was to increase their chances of succeeding in high school in the regular classroom, where grade-level reading was necessary to succeed. When thousands of schools nationwide can get this funding for their students, why couldn't the Placentia Unified School District not secure funding for a Title I program?

This school district needed to be made aware of the importance of such a program for disadvantaged kids. In fact, during my tenure at the high school, the board of education decided to eliminate a reading class from the curriculum of all junior high school students. After that, students from junior high schools came to the high schools with even lower reading scores than ever before. It was a district with school board members that fit the description Mark Twain once said about them. I'll let the reader look it up. It isn't flattering. Mistakes like this are also the result of mismanagement. The school district's administration, especially the assistant superintendent in charge of curriculum, should have made an effort to secure the reading program for students. Instead, the district administration allowed for eliminating reading classes at the seventh and eighth-grade levels. Sometimes, both educators and school board members fit the Mark Twain comment. In the meantime, the students suffer from not having a program that thousands of schools across the country have. I worked in a highly successful Title I program at Fullerton High School.

Because the school board and school administration didn't know what was happening in neighboring school districts, this is incredibly damaging to students. When a school district does not provide Title I funding for the district's junior highs and high schools, this is a severe oversight. I cannot understand why they were incapable of doing what the district right next to them was doing. The Placentia Yorba Unified School District needs Title I funding for their secondary schools, but they haven't learned of their importance. The district must use the funds to improve the reading abilities of disadvantaged students.

Title I reading labs work. I saw it firsthand at several schools. I created a reading "lab" in my room while teaching the reading classes at Valencia, but it could have been significantly funded if the district had applied for Title I funding. Despite not having the funding, I grew the program myself. The assessment used to measure their growth was the Nelson Reading Test I administered to my students. Their growth was also measured by taking the Comprehensive Test of Basic Skills to measure the language skill improvements of all students in Language Arts. It took a while to accomplish that goal, and about thirty percent of the funding for my program came from my pocket. The school administration and the district were so "out to lunch" that accomplishing such a task was beyond their scope. One wondered what any of these people did in the district office or why the school boards were not demanding better education for those disadvantaged kids. It could be because the school board members at the time represented the upper echelon of the school district, and no representation on the school board came from the disadvantaged kid's homes. If district administrators were to be curriculum leaders, they would have demonstrated that, especially when they allowed the school board to eliminate the reading class at the junior high schools.

A reading lab can save students from dropping out of school. We know the relationship between reading ability and incarceration. There is a deep relationship between the two. When there is no reading lab to assist students in improving their overall reading skills, it is a massive disservice to the community. I could not get anyone to address this issue at our school, and when they decided not to put me in charge of the reading department, I left the "reading department" and went to teach English instead. There are successful reading programs that a reading specialist often creates. I worked in a very successful program designed by a reading specialist. The program allowed students to focus on their reading skills and improve their language skills, as the language acquisition research indicated. Language acquisition is no secret. Reading is the basis for a good reading program.

Reading instruction is limited to the students who need to catch up to their classmates. All students should be engaged in reading instruction throughout their primary and secondary school years. We should establish what practices students must engage in to improve their reading skills. I once read that students were rarely able to read in school. The statistics on this are incredible. What was the teacher doing with time when they were in class? I allowed students to read in class for much of my career, but I discovered I was one of the rare teachers to do this.

I presented the idea to many of my colleagues about reading for fifteen minutes in their classrooms, but only some of them would allow their students to do that. I indicated that students could learn what was happening in the discipline they were studying. One economics teacher who allowed their students to read loved it because the students read the Wall

Street Journal in her class daily and asked questions she had not addressed in all the years she had taught. I advocated to many principals that students needed to read in every class for 15 minutes a day. Most of the time, this fell on deaf ears. Classes were 55 minutes long, and most students could not attend the instruction for fifty-five minutes anyway. By having students read, they could explore the subject they are learning another way. Schools should be advocates for reading and reading widely, not just fictional material.

A Title I reading program with a reading lab is a must at all high schools that qualify for it. It was an absolute disaster that our school, with an ever-increasing number of disadvantaged students, did not apply for the funding. It diminished students' performance for nearly thirty years and now sixteen more since my retirement. School districts can make significant errors like any other company, and the Placentia Unified School District had students miss out on a great opportunity.

Chapter 2:
Great English Departments Establish An Independent Reading Program

Dana Gioia indicated in a writing for the *National Endowment for the Arts,* "The daily reading habit, for instance, overwhelmingly correlates with better reading skills and higher academic achievement. On the other hand, poor reading skills correlate with lower levels of financial job success" (5,6). When an English department does not collectively establish an independent reading program, it misses an incredible opportunity to improve literacy. An independent reading program promotes outside reading and rewards students for doing that outside reading. Reading done during school and in the summer is all a part of an independent reading program. Despite the calls for it, the English department never established an independent reading program. The idea was just ignored because the thinking was that students would wait to do it anyway. My literacy grew exponentially in high school because of my independent reading there. I read eleven Steinbeck novels in my Chemistry class (I tell the story in my teaching memoir). As I indicated in the memoir, my high school demanded significant reading for our English courses. Besides the books I read independently, we read thirty-two works of literature over the four years of English instruction at La Habra High School from 1962-1966. While teaching at Valencia High School, only twenty percent of the honors students would read *Huckleberry Finn* when I assigned it. Some of the honors students stole the quizzes on the novel so they did not have to read the book.

In high school, my sophomore English teacher dropped a list of books to read on my desk (and everyone else's desk) with the words "Wake Up and Read!" I looked at the list and decided that this might be the best thing to do if I wanted to be prepared for and graduate from college. The list included about a hundred classic titles from World, American, and British literature. During those years, I attempted to read some of the novels on the list but found the reading difficult. It was more than problematic. The novels were over my head, both linguistically and historically. However, when I discovered a writer I enjoyed and could read without stopping every thirty seconds to look up a word, I read everything I could get my hands on by that author. I chose John Steinbeck and Ernest Hemingway and read as many of their novels as possible. Their effortless styles allowed me to increase my vocabulary because I could determine the meaning of the words in the context of the reading.

I was reading books and writers I could read, not Tolstoy, Turgenev, or Dostoevsky. I had to start where I was and discover what reading was accomplishable. In my junior year, I continued to read from the list but also had to read *The Scarlet Letter, Moby Dick, Huckleberry Finn, The Red Badge of Courage, and The Bridge of San Luis Rey* in my English classes during my junior year. Reading became a part of my life, and much was done independently. All it took was the encouragement of an English teacher to suggest that I independently read. In high school, the English teacher did not reward me for reading outside class or check to see if we were doing it. It was only a recommendation. However, I used the idea to encourage my students to read, and they did.

When I first became a teacher, I always had an independent reading program for my students. Promoting reading to my students was important since I was a reading teacher and a literature teacher. I set up the program from the beginning of the semester and asked that students read a book each quarter, and they would be awarded extra credit for doing so. I discussed the book with the students when they finished to be sure they read it. I learned how to determine if the student had read the book with critical questions about the story. I had over two hundred novels in my reading selection, and students checked them out from me to read. They had to replace it if they lost it. Although I was not privy to the curriculum of all English teachers, it was apparent that only a few established this kind of program in their classes. If they had done so, I would have heard about it from the students I had in my class. Students might say, "Oh, Ms. Elliot does this, too." However, students should have commented about an independent reading program in other classes. It was too bad that they did not encourage students to read independently since it is one of the Language Arts State Standards recommendations and one that I heartily agreed with. The state standards recommended that students read a million words during their four years of high school. Why were most of the teachers ignoring this recommendation?

The key to an independent reading program is knowing the reading levels of one's students and making sure that they are reading something within their range of vocabulary. I measured their vocabulary levels with the San Diego Quick Assessment. I was proficient at administering the test because I evaluated about three thousand students at Saddleback College while working in the reading lab there. It is an accurate test, and it gave me numbers that I could work with to properly place students in novels that were readable and accomplishable for them. Students enjoyed the fact that they were reading works that they could understand and that they could finish without giving up because the language was too difficult. Placing students randomly in books will only discourage students from reading.

This program taught me that linguistic skills can be improved if students read material within their range of reading. Professors argue that all literature should be presented to students regardless of reading level. In that case, those professors need to spend more time with students who reject books that are over their heads linguistically. Developing the skills to read more and more complex literature is a process that takes time. One must start with something other than Dostoevsky and develop language over time. Students need to be weaned from where they are and nudged up one step of the ladder each time they read a new book. Language takes time to acquire. Reading allows a student to play the "psycholinguistic guessing game," or the effort at determining the meaning of a word in the context within which it is read. The more the students challenge themselves, the quicker language is acquired. However, I only challenged them with language levels within their ability. I have seen students grow successfully with this approach, and I also learned to develop my language skills in high school with books I enjoyed without being overwhelmed by the language.

Because I advocated this approach to improving students' literacy, I saw test scores improve dramatically by the end of the year. As some readers may recall, the Comprehensive Test of Basic Skills (CTBS) was administered to our high school for quite a few years, and I was told that the students' most improved level was in the bottom quartile of the school. Those were my reading students. What did we do? Students read many books independently and in class, and I read to the class.

English departments must establish an independent reading program for the entire student body and determine how best to accomplish this goal. Students should be reading throughout their high school careers, and that means reading independently. The established program must be uniform throughout the four years of schooling.

An Independent Reading Program needs books. I kept all the books I read in high school and those I read in college. I also acquired many books as a reading teacher, so I had a library of two hundred books for students. I had determined that the books had three levels of reading difficulty: easy, medium, and challenging. I eventually learned how to label books according to their reading levels. This book reads at the 7th-grade level, and since my students were juniors and seniors, I labeled the book as easy. The first task is getting the books, which can come about by whatever means necessary to have a library extensive enough for the range of students in their classes.

The second task is to know the reading abilities of each student. What reading level ability does the student possess so the instructor can approve the student's reading selection? I sometimes had students who wanted to read books several grade levels above their reading level, and I did not allow them to do that. I would ask them if they wanted to be frustrated by the language of the book, and they would usually back off from wanting to read it. Knowing the reading levels of the books one has and the reading levels of the students is a crucial aspect of the reading program.

The third task is to determine how the student will be rewarded for reading the book since it is an independent reading program, and it is done by those motivated to do well in their English class. English teachers can make it an assignment per quarter or an extra-credit assignment. It was important that students manage to read a book a quarter and that it was part of their grade for the quarter.

The fourth task is to determine how to evaluate the student based on the reading they have done. If the student has read the entire book and a high degree of comprehension occurs, then a high grade is assigned. The students' evaluations took place when the students finished the book, and all evaluations had to be completed before the end of the quarter to assign a grade. If the student has finished two-thirds of the book, several points are awarded for that effort. Some students finished books rather quickly and needed another one before the end of the quarter; thus, an evaluation of a second book would result in extra credit.

The Independent Reading program can work in concert with the Sustained Silent Reading Program at school. Students are to read their independent books for the first 15 minutes of class—this way, they can finish the reading with class time and home time. Students should be encouraged to read their books between classes while waiting for instruction. I read a lot of pages waiting for classes to start when I was in high school. Students should be encouraged to do the same in the independent reading program.

Another characteristic of the Independent Reading Program is that the teacher can participate. English teachers should be seen reading a book and performing a "do as I do and not as I say." From time to time, the teacher can ask students what they are reading, and they share that with the class to draw interest in the book the student is reading. This motivates students to want to read the book they hear about. The teacher also shares what they are reading and why. Students want to know that the teacher is a reader, especially since they are English teachers.

Establishing an independent reading program for students is more critical than ever. Linguistic growth can only occur if students read hundreds of thousands of words to improve their linguistic abilities. The decline in overall literacy is the result of the avoidance of reading. Students need to read more than ever.

Chapter 3:
Great English Departments Have a Context-Based Vocabulary Program

When I say that English teachers are not reading teachers, I am saying they do not have the skills to improve the language mistakes that students make. They are not able to diagnose student reading problems. However, they are reading teachers in the sense that they improve students' language by encouraging the reading of literature and by attempting to improve their vocabulary. However, I'm afraid I have to disagree with random lists of vocabulary to improve students' language. A better context-based vocabulary program is a characteristic of a great English department.

English teachers think any random vocabulary list is sufficient for improving students' vocabulary. When these vocabulary words are selected, the vocabulary level that English teachers ask students to learn is often still being determined. These lists of vocabulary words can come from any source and may differ from the student's grade level. According to Dr. Timothy Rasinski of Kent State University, "Inadequate vocabulary acquisition is very likely one of the reasons that U.S. student reading has not progressed for the last 30 years despite numerous national and state literacy initiatives." (Learning A-Z.com) A good deal of that inadequate vocabulary expansion can be attributed to teachers who teach random lists of words. Vocabulary is best learned in the context of the reading one does. A well-planned vocabulary development program is a hallmark of a great English department.

We all know that vocabulary expands when one reads. The reader is playing the "psycholinguistic guessing game" by trying to determine the meaning of words in the context of the reading. The more often students choose a word's definition based on its context, the more quickly their language develops. Students can read and determine the meaning of words based on the context of the reading. The students' language will grow if they participate in the Independent Reading Program.

English teachers may be offended by the previous argument that they are not reading teachers because they teach vocabulary. The question is, what vocabulary do they teach? English teachers think any random vocabulary list is sufficient for improving students' vocabulary. There is no certainty about the vocabulary level that English teachers ask students to learn. These lists of vocabulary words can come from any source, but the most crucial aspect is whether the vocabulary has anything to do with their reading. A good deal of that inadequate vocabulary expansion can be attributed to teachers who teach lists of words in isolation from reading. Vocabulary is best learned in the context of the reading one does.

We all know that vocabulary improves when one reads. The reader is playing the "psycholinguistic guessing game" by trying to determine the meaning of words in the context of the reading. So, rather than a list of isolated words that have no inherent meaning to the students except for the definition that is told to them by the teacher, it is essential to teach the words in the story as the story is read. In other words, it teaches students that learning vocabulary is accomplished by reading the sentence that gives it meaning. Students were thrown off when I taught vocabulary that way because they had been studying vocabulary in isolation for many years. Over time, their growth as readers improved as they continued to study vocabulary in the context of their readings. This is why English teachers are not reading teachers; the reading masters tells those who have taken the degree that vocabulary in context is best for literacy growth. As Dr. Rasinski indicated, our literacy growth has decreased over the last thirty years partly because of this practice.

Another way to ensure vocabulary growth is to teach the vocabulary word in the sentence students will read in the literary work. This is teaching vocabulary. Teaching vocabulary as it is used in the sentence provides the meaning it has as a result of its context. This program should be established for the four years of required reading students will do for their English classes. If a 9th-grade class is reading *Romeo and Juliet*, teaching essential words from the play is vital. Testing the students can be part of the overall test of the play, or quizzes on the vocabulary from each act can be administered. In other words, students learn vocabulary by reading the sentence that gives it meaning. Students were thrown off when I taught vocabulary that way because they had been studying vocabulary by lists of words thrown at them for many years.

Over time, their growth as readers improved as they continued to study vocabulary in the context of their readings. English teachers mistakenly believe that teaching a list of vocabulary each week improves their students' vocabulary. While it does, to some degree, it is less effective than setting up vocabulary from the literature students read. If teaching vocabulary lists was so effective, why did literacy decline? As Dr. Rasinski indicated, our literacy growth has decreased over the last thirty years partly because of this practice.

Seeing vocabulary in rich contexts provided by authentic texts rather than isolated vocabulary drills produces robust vocabulary learning (National Reading Panel, 2000). As a reading instructor, I learned that teaching vocabulary in the context of the readings one is doing improves vocabulary knowledge better than an isolated list of vocabulary words. The two approaches differ significantly, and English teachers champion teaching isolated words.

The standard approach to "teaching" a vocabulary list is to introduce the words at the beginning of the week, then have students study the words for a "practice" test on Wednesday and then a final graded test on Friday. In the meantime, students must use the words in a sentence and submit their work on the test day. The test would consist of matching the words with their definitions. Students with good memories are apt to do better than those who cannot remember as well. This process is produced each week throughout the year. Students think they are getting smarter studying these words in isolation. Words only have meaning once they are used in a sentence, and so the practice of teaching them words in isolation from the reading is almost fruitless. To keep with the theme of this book, it punctuates the other teaching in the classroom. It interrupts the learning in the school, which is more significant.

The irony of teaching "lists" of vocabulary is that they are randomly selected and may not even be at grade level for students. I saw a set of vocabulary words for a freshman honors class that was sure to be at the 14th-grade level or the sophomore-in-college reading level. For what reason does the English teacher think that a list of vocabulary words that are several grade levels about the reading level of the best of 9th-grade honors students? It is a fruitless task that creates unnecessary chaos in the class and interrupts the teaching otherwise. It is part of the reason the appearance of teaching English is so hodgepodge.

Teaching vocabulary to English classes throughout the school should be consistent. The English teachers should create the program in committees for the different grade levels. The vocabulary should come from the readings, and learning the vocabulary should occur in the context of the reading. Words have meaning when used in a sentence, not sitting isolated on a shelf waiting for a meaning. If vocabulary is taught in the context of the reading, then vocabulary learning is enhanced. Teaching vocabulary in the context of the readings is more valuable to linguistic growth than learning words in isolation from the reading.

Chapter 4:
Great English Departments Have English Teachers Who Know Reading

The ultimate irony of becoming an English teacher is the assumption on the part of the public that English teachers are teachers of reading. Technically, they are not teachers of reading. They are teachers of literature, the reading that they make students do. However, English teachers do not know how to teach reading, but they do teach literature and the language of literature. They are, for the most part, teachers of reading literature. There is a big difference between a reading teacher and a literature teacher, and the purpose here is to show that being prepared to teach literature does not make an English teacher a teacher of reading.

Reading teachers assess the reading skills of their students at the beginning of the semester and the end of the semester. English teachers don't. Reading teachers teach vocabulary in the context of its use. English teachers don't. Reading teachers focus on improving the comprehension of their students. English teachers do so sometimes, but only sometimes. Reading teachers know about readability. English teachers need to learn about readability for the most part. Some do. Reading teachers know how to measure the language level of a book. English teachers don't. Reading teachers understand what works best to improve a student's reading ability. English teachers need to learn how to improve a student's reading ability.

A reading teacher concentrates on improving students' vocabulary and comprehension. A reading teacher also encourages readable reading materials, not unreadable, as some literature can be. Some will argue that allowing students to read complex literature is beneficial to improving their language, but I don't believe that. In other words, some argue that reading complex literature for students, regardless of their reading levels, is acceptable. Students gain literacy by being challenged by the reading instead of being overwhelmed.

English teachers could teach comprehension better. It is important to evaluate students' reading by asking them questions about the reading. Reading literature is complex, and asking questions about the reading determines their comprehension level. It should be a standard to ask students what they learned about the reading through a series of comprehension questions. Reading chapters in a novel should be followed with questions about the reading. Reading poetry should be followed by a series of questions to clarify misunderstandings about the reading of the poem, and so on. Comprehension questions can be simple to complex. All levels of questioning should be put to the students to increase their understanding of the deeper issues of the reading. This is what standardized testing evaluates.

English teachers need to learn about readability. Readability is how easy or difficult it is to read something. The irony of teaching literature is that the readability levels of the literature are not identified. For example, what is *To Kill a Mockingbird's* reading (or readability) level? Although there is an approximate reading level, the exact reading levels of literature are not identified by reading measures. A book can be measured for its readability using several readability formulas. This is not the domain of the English teacher. English teachers do not get degrees in reading; their degrees are in literature. There are ways to determine the readability level of the books teachers ask students to read. All literature should have identified reading levels assigned to the book. *The Scarlet Letter* should be labeled an eleventh-grade reading-level book before students begin to read it. Since we have already discussed the reading levels, we must know how well a student reads before assigning books to them. This is especially important for the independent reading students should be required to do during their courses in English. English teachers can only measure the student's reading abilities at the beginning of the class. This was discussed in the chapter on assessment. If English teachers are going to teach so much literature, then it would be nice to know if students grow linguistically from it.

Readability measures how easy or hard a book is to read. For example, *To Kill a Mockingbird* has been measured to read at the 10th-grade level. The book is taught in the sophomore year, so it is appropriately placed for students reading at grade level when they enter the class. In other words, a student who enters the sophomore year should be reading at a 10.0-grade level, meaning the combination of the student's vocabulary and comprehension ability as measured by the Nelson-Denny reading test would be 10.0. By the end of the year, the student will have grown a full year linguistically and can read at the 11.0 level at the beginning of the junior year and

12.0 at the start of the senior year. Knowing the readability of a reading is essential.

Students who are behind linguistically need additional work on their language to catch up with what is considered to be grade-level reading. Without going into the causes of the decline of linguistic abilities, it suffices to say that English teachers are ill-equipped to improve the reading skills of students who have fallen behind. Students who are behind need additional work, which is the job of the reading teacher in a reading lab. Students need to forgo an elective and take an extra class in reading development to improve their reading to grade level.

Reading aloud to students is a must. English teachers think this is inappropriate, but it must be corrected. The language of students in high school is still developing, and it can be enhanced significantly by reading to them. Then, students can read aloud because the teacher modeled how to read something aloud. It is interesting to see how students know words they may not have ever known because I have already read them aloud. English teachers do not always think developing "reading skills" in an English class is important, but ironically, they are the source of students' reading and writing skills. Learning the pace and rhythm of reading is another benefit of reading aloud to students. The pace and rhythm of reading need to be modeled, and students can quickly adapt to reading aloud if it is modeled well. Students need to read aloud and learn to articulate the language in front of them. I never wanted to embarrass a student who could not read well out loud, so I gave them an out. They could skip the reading aloud in class but had to read to me during the reading time or when they could see me before school or during lunch. It was only a five-minute reading, but they had to do it at some point.

English teachers take a minor amount of coursework in teaching reading. It isn't sufficient to teach them everything a master's degree in reading does, but it conveys that reading is essential. Additional coursework in teaching reading should be part of an English teacher's training. Knowing how language is acquired will influence how English teachers teach. English teachers should be reading, writing, and literature majors, not just literature majors. Learning enough about these three skills can help improve their students' literacy more significantly than the approach perpetuated for decades.

Part B:
Writing Hallmarks

Chapter 5:
Great English Departments Have an Established Writing Program

In the opening of my book *Confessions of an English Teacher: A Memoir of My Teaching Years*, a quote by Parker J. Pilmer hits the nail on the head: "Teaching is perhaps the most privatized of all the public professions. Though we teach in front of students, we always teach solo, out of collegial sight—as contrasted with surgeons and lawyers who work in the presence of others who know their craft well. When we walk into our workplace, the classroom, we close the door on our colleagues. When we emerge, we rarely talk about what happened or what needs to happen next, for we have no shared experience to talk about." In other words, we don't know what happens in the classroom unless we watch our colleagues teach because we do not share our teaching experiences. We must break that mold of isolation from each other's teaching and organize the program for our students. Great English departments have an organized writing program.

The English department staff should design an English department writing program to ensure continuity in the writing students do in preparation for college. It is a mistake not to organize the writing for students, which essentially prepares them for college. A couple of things are essential for the student who wishes to get a college education, and English departments can be helpful. English departments should teach writing that students will find in their college classes. For example, a Modern Language Association paper should be taught to all students since most colleges expect students to write this essay. Teaching this paper to students prepares them for the expectations of learning at the college level.

A writing program should be a coordinated effort to outline the writing students will do during their four years in high school. While it is not the purview of this writing to tell the English departments what writings to establish, some parameters are necessary. It is highly recommended that the MLA-style paper be assigned for all four years. It is a Common Core requirement. It wasn't reassuring for me to learn that my old high school had abandoned the teaching of this paper. All students who are in a college-bound class should be learning to write this paper. The paper should be short in the first year and successively longer each following year. The MLA handbook should be a staple in the English department for all students to use while they write their papers. The documented research paper can either be an argumentative or expository writing. This will be the format for all writings in the humanities when taking a college degree. The APA-style research paper format is used in education, psychology, and science. This paper should be taught in the social science department. If one learns the MLA-style format, the APA style is slightly different, and students will adapt. The Chicago/Turabian style is generally used in Business, History, and the Fine Arts.

At the last high school where I taught, all four levels of classes were to have the students write an MLA-style argumentative paper before the end of the school year. The requirements of the paper escalated as students went from one grade level to the next. The freshmen paper was only three pages long, the sophomore paper four pages or maybe five, the junior paper was to be more than five pages, and the senior wrote a ten-page paper. All of these papers required different numbers of sources to use in the paper to bolster their arguments about a controversial topic. The senior English teachers were excellent at administering and requiring the students to write the paper and teaching them how to do it. It was a terrific success, and many students went off to college with the ability to put together an MLA-style paper, taking a position on an argumentative subject.

Aside from the research paper, English teachers should be teaching the literary paper. Teaching literary papers is something the English teacher should have learned when taking a degree in literature. The English degree requires a great many documents about literary works. Some books help English teachers teach literary papers. The standard in my day was the book *Writing About Literature* by Edgar V. Roberts, which could have been better. It did not speak to the kinds of essays students would write in high school and was more suited to the papers students would do at the college level. I would not allow my students to buy it because I did not want to teach the kinds of literary papers the author had shown to teach. If one wants to know how people feel about the book, look at the comments on the one-star ratings on Amazon. "The book wastes 50.00 dollars," one English teacher said.

Critically, English teachers need an excellent source to teach literary papers. English teachers must buy it themselves and somehow transfer the knowledge from the book to the students; we all know what a challenge that is. However, if one chooses to do this, several books can help teach students to write literary papers. *Reading and Writing about Literature: A Portable Guide* by Janet E. Gardner; *A Short Guide to Writing about Literature* by Sylvan Barnet; *A Writer's Reference with Writing about Literature* by Diana Hacker and Nancy Sommers; *Writing about Literature: A Guide for the Student Critic* by W.F. Garrett-Petts and *How to Write a Literature Review: Purpose, Process and Practical Guidance* by Dr. Matthew Vollrath and Dr. Robert Lloyd. Students can benefit from a good resource for writing a literary paper.

I designed my lessons to teach students to write those papers. I had students write on the same topic, but they used their style to present the information. The whole writing process was exercised to teach students how to take an idea to a completed paper. I taught the reading process with the writing process. I taught them how to incorporate a literary work into their writing. In this regard, an English teacher can teach writing. They can teach how writing is supposed to be done if they do it together. In the past, too much of the teaching of writing relied on the students doing it themselves. This is not teaching writing. This is assigning writing. When we read, especially literature, we draw conclusions that essentially become our papers' thesis. Showing students how to draft a thesis is teaching writing. Showing students how to support the thesis is teaching writing. Showing students how to exercise the writing process while writing a paper is teaching writing. In that regard, English teachers can teach writing. It has been said that writing cannot be taught, but I disagree.

English teachers should know about the different forms of writing: expository, narrative, descriptive, and argumentative. However, an examination of what is valuable to students when we teach them writing has yet to be made. There are no definitive writings that students do, and even when one requires them, the English teacher closes the door and does their own thing anyway. Unfortunately, English teachers act like independent contractors who answer to no one. If they get along with the powers that be, they are secure in doing whatever they like. If they cause trouble, they are more scrutinized and criticized like a social pariah. I have seen excellent English teachers "fired" or let go by the administration because they did good things in the classroom that diverged from the mundane idiocy of the long past. I learned not to open my mouth and ask questions until after my tenure. I had tenure when I opened my mouth and criticized the Senior Poetry Project that English teachers had been doing for ten years at the school, which was essentially a literary piece of garbage. Deciding on what kinds of papers are essential to the students is a matter of researching the colleges the students will attend. Those college English departments are more than happy to share what they expect of students who will attend their colleges.

The general argument in this chapter is that the teaching of writing could be more organized for better overall results. There needed to be more consistency in the selection of writing in all of the schools where I taught. It was too much of a "do-your-own-thing" approach to teaching writing. For those students who were lucky enough to have English teachers who had worked at learning how to teach writing, they improved. However, for those teachers who did not know how to approach the teaching of writing, the students suffered. When I checked my students' portfolios in my junior classes, I saw they had two years of writing, and very little, if any, of the writing was the MLA-style research paper. This paper would serve them well as writers during their entire college career. Yet, these English teachers ignored teaching it. It may be too much trouble for them to teach, or they may need to be made aware of how to teach it. And they may need to learn the style better. They did not want to embarrass themselves without knowing what to do and how to teach it.

By planning the English department programs together, English teachers can positively impact students' literacy growth. With a well-planned writing program for each grade level, the students' writing literacy improves over their four years in high school.

Chapter 6:
Great English Departments
Teach Writing as a Process

If an English teacher has yet to learn that the teaching of writing has changed, then they are missing out. Teaching writing has a new approach: writing needs to be taught as a process. I am basing my judgment on what I saw and learned about other English teachers teaching writing. What I saw when I worked at six different high schools was disheartening. Many English teachers did not teach writing as a process because they had yet to receive much instruction about how to do that. Since they received no instruction about teaching writing in their preparatory classes for teaching English, they did not exercise the process in class. Frequently, I saw teachers assigning writing assignments and not teaching students to write by exercising the writing process with them. As an English teacher, I saw that I needed to learn to teach writing in general and mainly teach students how to exercise writing as a process.

It is best to teach students how to write using the writing process by making the class do the same paper before they venture out and write their essays independently. Although we do not necessarily want our students to go through a lock-step process to perform writing, a systematic approach can benefit them initially. Since I can only conclude from my observations of English teachers about writing, I learned that many needed more training to teach the writing process. During the twenty-six years I taught at one high school, it would have been an excellent topic of discussion for an English department meeting. Yet, as the reader may know from my earlier writing, we did no such thing. We broke into grade-level groups and discussed the issues teaching our grade levels. If we had senior classes, we sat with the others who taught seniors and debated issues teaching that grade level. Even in those groups, we did not discuss teaching writing as a process. If we did talk about teaching students to use a method of creating writing, it was by accident rather than on purpose.

The question important to teaching writing is whether we are assigning or teaching writing. Teaching writing is coaxing the students through the process of writing a paper. That is what teaching writing is. In my high school days, we were "assigned" an essay to write, and after submitting the paper, the English tore it apart like a wild animal only to expose all the "blood" (red ink) all over the paper when we received it back with two grades at the top of the paper. One was for the content of the paper, and the other was for the grammar and mechanics of the paper. There were no rewrites of the paper. There was no feedback on the paper before it was submitted. There was no generation of ideas for the writing. There was nothing but an assignment. The evaluation of the essay ended the "process" of writing the paper. College writing was the same experience, with professors assigning papers to be written and then evaluating them with the same metric of "editing" the paper, "exposing" the problems with the arguments not made in the paper, and identifying grammatical concerns. English professors were not writing teachers but writing critics. They evaluated the paper using the same approach as my high school teachers. They rarely submitted comments that taught students how to improve their writing.

What is teaching writing as a process? The goal is to get the students to work the paper like a professional does when writing. A professional goes through the process of deciding what to write about, limiting the writing scope, writing a rough draft, getting feedback on the writing, revising, and repeating the cycle a couple more times. While writing one of my books, I went through four drafts before settling on the final draft as the book. The initial draft had numerous revisions; the writing process was exercised on the second, third, and fourth drafts. That process was exercised on two hundred-page books. Although the process can vary a bit, the understanding is that students need to work on a paper like a professional instead of drafting a paper without exercising the process.

Teaching writing as a process is essential for the growth of the student writer. They need to learn to generate their ideas, organize them in an outline, draft a rough draft, and then receive feedback about the rough draft. When I was at Fullerton High School, we learned how to conference with students about their writing through a program at Huntington Beach High School District. Their teachers worked with Ross Winterowd of the University of Southern California to improve their writing teaching. I was a part of what would be considered the beginning of teaching composition as a process. Although Professor Winterowd was going in the right direction, there would be a lot of changes in the teaching of writing over the next three decades. All English departments should have been involved in this evolution. As an English department, in the twenty-six years I was there, the English department leadership never led a single discussion on teaching writing as a process.

English teachers should be a group of people learning from each other about how to teach composition to their students. When I was at Fullerton High School, we discussed the teaching of composition all the time as we learned more and more from the work of Ross Winterowd. Learning and teaching English is an ongoing matter, and from the perspective of an English teacher who has spent many years in different high school and college environments, there is a long way to go. I write these books to make a difference by asking people in the community of colleges to prepare English teachers to teach writing.

I started teaching in an era when teaching writing was not even a subject at the college level. It was not on any professor's radar, and taking a degree in the teaching of writing was a long way away. Over the years I have taught, writing has become more focused at the college and research level. Literacy was declining, so what would we do about teaching writing better? (I believe literacy was declining because more generations were reading less than their predecessors and engaging in activities like Facebook). I learned very early that I did not know how to teach writing, and I was not taught much as a student teacher by my master English teachers.

All professional writers get feedback on their writing. Professors who write books ask their colleagues to give feedback on the books or articles they write for professional journals. I have read nearly twenty-five books by a University of North Carolina professor. I wrote to him each time I read another of his books and indicated where the copy editors missed the errors. He appreciated my observations while reading his books, but I also learned much about the writing process from him. He shared his writing process with his followers. I knew that writing is not done in a vacuum but in cooperation with others who see the book differently than the author so that the author presents his best writing forward for it to be published. Publishing comes long after the feedback and editing work are done.

If teaching writing as a process is not discussed in English department meetings, then the department chair should be replaced. Writing requires using a process, and teaching students to exercise it will make them more capable of writing better essays. It is a fundamental hallmark of a great English department. These are the books I recommend to learn writing as a process: *Draft No. 4: On the Writing Process* by John McPhee; *On Writing: A Memoir of the Craft* by Stephen King; *Crack the Essay: Secrets of Argumentative Writing Revealed* by Simon Black.

Chapter 7:
Great English Departments Have a Consistent Writing Evaluation Program

There is a history to the evaluation of English papers. In my day in high school, my English teachers gave us an assignment to write an essay on a literary topic. There was no teaching of the essay, but only parameters were given for the writing: it must be three pages, double-spaced, and typed. After we had written the essays, the English teachers would evaluate the papers and return them in two weeks. There would be two grades at the top of the paper: content and grammar. Also, the English teacher had "spilled" red ink all over the paper, indicating where the student had gone wrong in grammar, spelling, and mechanics. B-/C+ would be the grade for the assignment. This is how English teachers graded essays for their students in the 1960s, 1970s, and 1980s. My master teacher used the same evaluation tool in the early 1970s.

In college, when I got my papers back from the professors in the English department, there was a grade at the top and a comment. There were errors identified in the writing, but only sometimes. It depended on whether the professor wanted to take the night off from "editing" the paper. So, in those early years of evaluating the papers, I did the same thing: I identified the errors as best I could, and I assessed the paper based on content and proper English usage and mechanics (use of punctuation, spelling, and capitalization). It was highly speculative. It was a system. I had to justify a grade on the paper. Did it help my students become better writers? No. I knew I did not know enough about teaching writing to make a difference in those days. It would take more education.

As time passed, rubrics were introduced as a method of evaluating papers. Rubrics are multidimensional sets of scoring guidelines that can be used to evaluate student work consistently. They spell out scoring criteria so that multiple teachers, using the same rubric for a student's essay, would arrive at the same score or grade. The irony of the rubric is that not all English teachers use them, nor do they use them consistently; therefore, evaluation, at best, is inconsistent. Because there is a great deal of inconsistency in evaluating essays, it is one of the "bitter pills" students take away from the English class.

When we had research papers written, evaluation forms were made to evaluate the writing. It was more work than the students were putting in doing the paper! The writing evaluation must be more consistent to prevent English teachers from looking idiotic. What one teacher was doing to evaluate papers was not what another person in the next classroom was doing to assess his or her student's paper, and the whole process made the profession of English teachers look like the Keystone Cops running around the car trying to find which door to enter to get this thing right. There was no consistency in the evaluation of the essay, so how do you think students felt when a paper was an "A" in one class and a "C" in another? It was just the beginning of an absolute nightmare of teaching English—the inconsistency in evaluating papers using rubrics.

This chapter will highlight the problem I experienced watching teachers evaluate papers. One conclusion I came to about English departments was that too many needed to be on the same page regarding evaluation. When an English department evaluates a perfectly written paper with a range of "A" to "F," work must be done. English departments need to organize the evaluations of each assigned paper at each grade level so students can see them as someone who know what they are doing.

This story illustrates that English teachers need a handle on how papers are supposed to be evaluated. They are all over the place when evaluating compositions written by students. The evaluation systems used by English teachers varied, so students needed clarification about how papers should be evaluated. This kind of inconsistency was professionally wrong. It appeared that English teachers did not know what they were doing, and the fact of the matter was they did not. They need better education about the evaluation of papers. Since writing is so personal and evaluation systems are poor, we make many enemies teaching writing because we are not competent enough to evaluate it. Teaching the subject of writing is still in the dark ages today because of the inconsistency of its education.

During my first year teaching at a high school, a group of teachers sat around in a department meeting with the task of reading an essay presented by a student to one of the teachers' classes. We were all asked to assign a grade for the paper. About fifteen teachers were sitting in a circle, and at the end of the evaluation, the department chair asked each of us to tell the rest of the English teachers what grade they had given to the paper. Some of us gave the paper an "A," while some gave it a "B," and others gave it a "C." One teacher arrived at the "D" level, but the most interesting was a rather arrogant teacher who assigned the paper an "F." The different teachers gave their reasonings for the grade. They were random and far-fetched reasons. Each English teacher read the paper differently and gave interesting comments about what they saw in the paper.

The teacher who arrived at the "F" grade said the paper was "too pretentious." Can one imagine that? Here was a teacher who did not even consider the writing itself. The paper was well organized, with a good beginning, middle, and end. The paper had perfect mechanics, spelling, and grammar. Yet, he read it as a pretentious piece of writing. He felt the writer was not taking the writing seriously, so he thought it best to give it an "F." How is that affecting a student's view of the English teacher? I heard stories at different parties about people's experiences with writing evaluations. I would hear the horror stories of those who found English teachers to be a bizarre kind of creature. Several of them earned it.

To further add to this legacy of the English teacher, I was in the doctor's office the other day, and he asked me what I had done for a living. I told him I was an English teacher. "Whoa, boy, that was something I'll never forget." I asked him what he was referring to, and he said, "My English teacher wrote at the top of my paper, 'Such a brilliant analysis of the story. I'm very impressed.'" My doctor added that the grade at the top of the paper was a C+. I laughed when he said that because I was writing this book about the teaching of writing at the time of the visit to his office. I then quickly told him the story of the English teacher who gave an "F" to a perfectly written paper. Is there something wrong here?

I confess that I was never trained in college to evaluate papers by the English or education departments. When English teachers take courses in the education program, they take courses from professors with degrees in education. The Doctor of Education is a research or professional doctoral program focusing on education. The program's students may focus on degrees in administration in education, clinical studies, research on issues in education, curriculum work, leadership, or running public institutions. It is rare to see an education professor whose focus is on the teaching of English. Instead, the education department hires a former English teacher with a master's degree in English who teaches a "methods" course. This course might teach prospective English teachers to focus on a topic like grammar or some literature subject. However, the education department does not teach English teachers how to evaluate essays. The course is a two-unit course and is not considered to be a serious course. This is the course where English teachers are supposed to learn how to teach English, and it is mostly to blame for why English teachers arrive in the classroom so woefully unprepared to teach English. This includes the teaching of writing.

When I took the course in education, I found it to be completely worthless. The courses had no classroom application because the course should have taught us how to teach aspects of English, like teaching grammar, literature, composition, spelling, and vocabulary. The course did none of these. Without going too far in my indictment of the Education department, most courses are a total waste of time. Many of those education professors think they are doing something constructive for English teachers when, most of the time, they are wasting their time on nonsense courses.

I could see how poorly prepared English teachers were at evaluating essays through our "portfolio" system introduced to the English department. Teachers passed their students' portfolios on to their next English teacher. When I examined these portfolios, evaluating essays and other papers was random and varied widely. In other words, how an essay was assessed in the freshman year would differ markedly from the evaluation in the junior year. It is no wonder that the students remark about the weirdness and wildness of the English teacher's assessment of their writings. Some papers had a grade at the top without a single comment and no indication that the paper had even been read. No wonder English teachers want to close their doors and not expose to other English teachers or, more significantly, to the public what they are doing. One English teacher I observed never carried anything home to grade. Somehow, he managed to "evaluate" papers without any comments or feedback, but only a letter grade at the top.

In the early days of my teaching, I learned a system of evaluating essays from my master teacher, who assigned two grades at the top of the paper, one for content and one for grammar. I used that system for many years and rarely got questioned by the student about the overall grade, which was a combination of the two marks. In those early days of teaching, I marked the errors (essentially edited them) on the essays my students submitted until I learned that these corrections made no difference in improving a student's writing. When I used this evaluation system, the review was never challenged.

There were several causes for how we ended up with so many variations in evaluation. First, it is the English teacher's independent contractor approach to teaching the subject, and every English teacher "knows best." Behind those closed doors, the English teacher dismantles the writing ego of students one at a time. They issue "Fs" for essays perfectly written because they don't know anything about the teaching of writing. Because teachers do not collaborate on evaluating the writing students do, there are different evaluations for the same assigned paper. It all depends on how the teacher sees the paper with the evaluation tool they devise. It is this attitude that allows English teachers to do whatever they want when it comes to the evaluation of essays. That is why when confronted at parties by people who learn English, they immediately refer to the randomness of evaluating their writing. A second complaint usually was about literature and its interpretation of it. That is a whole different story.

Another important reason for this randomness is the need for more effective leadership. Poor leadership allows for this wild variation in the evaluation of papers. There is no reason why consistent evaluation of writing assigned at different grade levels should not exist. If the department's leadership does not evaluate essays as an important topic at department meetings, then the department chair is derelict in performing the position's duties.

If the writing education of teachers were better, then they might not make grievous mistakes. I attribute the poor understanding of the teaching of writing to the inadequate education English teachers get in preparation for teaching. This does not include everyone's experience, but it covers most new teachers. I question where the English teacher is learning about the history of rhetoric and where that education exists. I cannot imagine why English teachers are not taught the history of argumentation and the basis for argumentation in a writing class for an English degree. I attribute this to the fact that few English professors specialize in the history of rhetoric. They love their literature and prefer to be scholars who teach a particular author, which is how they earn their Ph.D.

An equal cause for the failure of the teaching of writing is that English departments fail to create the assignments and the evaluation tools together. I am not saying that all English departments have this issue. Some English departments do all and more of what I have outlined in this book, and so I am not saying it isn't done at all. I have seen English departments with their act together. My kids went to University High School in Irvine. The school sends about ten students to Stanford every year, and it is a top-rated academic high school in California and the country. All one has to do is look at the English department website and see great organization. While researching the school on the internet, I found a former Stanford student who reviewed the school: "I had a phenomenal experience in my four years at University High, ultimately getting into Stanford as a President's scholar along with nine of my classmates. The student body was filled with some of the smartest, most dedicated people I know, whom I am still close with to this day. The teachers were always top-notch and noble and loved what they did. I could not have had a better experience and would highly recommend it." My kids used to say college was "easier" than attending University High School. University High School was academically rigorous. One of my kids went to Stanford, and the other went to UC Santa Barbara. The University High School English department is one of those that organizes what they teach.

Writing evaluation is an important part of an English department, but more departments should take it seriously. These inconsistencies confuse students, who end up telling stories to retired English teachers about how their English teacher abused them through the mismanagement of their writing evaluations.

Chapter 8:
Great English Departments Know How to Teach Grammar

The traditional approach to the teaching of grammar has a long history. Grammar's history includes teaching grammar from a textbook for as long as I can remember. It was believed that teaching grammar improves students' writing skills. After many years of research and examination, it has been determined that teaching grammar in isolation from writing is a complete waste of time. Isolated grammar teaching has a deleterious effect on the writing of students. In other words, writing got worse before it got better. Therefore, grammar teaching should be done so in the context of a student's writing and not in isolation from the writing.

It was in the early 1980s that I learned of the waste of time that teaching grammar was. George Hillocks, Jr.'s study at the University of Chicago called "What Works in Teaching Composition: A Meta-analysis of Experimental Treatment Studies" indicated that all the grammar in the world does not improve a student's writing. In short, he concluded that grammar exercises like quizzes on parts of speech and naming types of phrases, clauses, and sentences made writing worse instead of better. It would be the second most crucial understanding of my career as an English teacher. While grammar is vital in the proper context, it alone does not make a writer become a better writer. Grammar is the linguistic understanding of the language. Writing improves with reading and writing and not with the study of the linguistics of language.

The wasted time teaching grammar from a textbook was validated later in my career when I was a student at the University of California at Irvine, studying how to teach writing. Aside from the study by George Hillocks, other professors claimed that grammar hinders writing development rather than helps it. Patricia A. Dunn, professor of English at Stony Brook University in New York, wrote an essay titled "Teaching Grammar Improves Writing," where she comments, "Teaching grammar improves students' knowledge of linguistics. But if students' writing is to improve, teachers need to teach writing" (144). Further in the essay, she states, "For more than fifty years, researchers have studied how teaching traditional grammar (parts of speech, names of phrases and clauses, types of sentences, etc.) has affected student writing. The results have been consistent: Writing does not improve and sometimes worsens after grammar instruction. To see a meta-analysis of the studies that show these results, start with George Hillocks's 1986 book, *Research on Written Composition: New Directions for Teaching*. His 1987 article in Educational Leadership, 'Synthesis of Research on Teaching Writing,' is a shortened version of his book, and a chart on page seventy-five of that article shows which approaches to teaching writing work better than others" (148). When I was teaching in the early 70s, I was unaware of these studies, but through my study of writing in the mid to late 1980s, I discovered the research that changed my perspective on teaching grammar. Unfortunately, I could not change the system that continued to mandate the teaching of it in traditional ways: with worksheets. Try to tell some schoolmarm that teaching grammar has nothing to do with improving the students' writing. I know. I tried. Once, I told a college instructor who had taught grammar for forty years that grammar instruction has no discernible impact on improving writing. He looked at me with a wide open mouth and said, "That's impossible." I didn't argue with him. I did not want to disparage his life's work.

Grammar must be taught in collaboration with writing because there is no transfer or understanding of the learning away from writing. While the goal is not to convince the reader of the waste of time that teaching grammar away from writing is, the goal is to convince the reader that grammar is best taught when students have writing in hand. Sentences with misplaced modifiers can also be indicated to the student with a grammar program. Any grammar program that identifies the misuse of the language is valuable in teaching the student how to place language effectively. Students need to work with their sentences to learn grammar. Modifications to sentences teach students how grammar works. Students learn how grammar works if they rewrite sentences in their writing.

Grammar can be learned with sentence combining. Combining a couple of sentences a student has written teaches more complex sentence structure and teaches them to vary the types of sentences they use. I would ask students to alter the sentences in their writing to use complex and compound structures to communicate their ideas. Using writing that a student has already created will allow students to learn more sophisticated writing patterns and complexity in communication. Teaching grammar from a textbook will not enable students to see the benefit of better sentence construction if they have their own sentences.

During my career, I taught a lot of grammar, mainly at the community college level and less at the high school level. When students entered community colleges in the areas near their high schools, they were evaluated for English placement at the colleges with a grammar test. English departments at the community colleges assumed that students who did not know grammar could not write well. There was at least one of two prerequisite courses for students who had "failed" the English grammar placement test. In other words, they did not know grammar well, so they were denied entrance into freshman English and were forced to take English A for an entire semester and then English B for a full semester before entering freshman English.

English A was a total grammar course. The irony is that students who scored low on the placement test were forced to take a year of English, English A, and English B. Both courses required learning vast amounts of grammar. The research that clearly shows the ill effects of teaching grammar to students has yet to be understood and applied even in today's community colleges. A student can enter any nearby community college in California and have vast amounts of grammar taught to them to "remediate" their writing. Unfortunately, because this has been the traditional approach that English teachers have taken to remediate students' poor writing, nothing has changed despite all the research showing it is fruitless to do so. If one wants to improve the student's English abilities, writing is that vehicle, not grammar.

The best approach to improving grammar and writing is with reading. If an English teacher wants to improve a student's writing, have them read something and write about what they are reading. Language growth happens through the acquisition of it by reading and then by writing about the reading. The irony is that English teachers became much more literate by doing precisely that: reading and writing about literature. The result was greater literacy. Instead of having students read and write about their reading, they feed them large amounts of grammar to improve their literacy. The system perpetuates the mistake because no one is powerful enough to change it. The same textbooks are used in these low-level English classes and are grammar texts that drill students into nausea.

An even greater irony is that research goes way back that demonstrates this fact: grammar damages one's writing abilities instead of enhancing them. Why has this research been ignored? Far too many English teachers believe that grammar study improves writing. English teachers need to take courses in reading or studying how someone acquires language. I once told a Ph.D. professor who teaches English as a Second Language that teaching grammar to second-language students wastes time. She nearly had a heart attack on the spot. I told her that reading was the way to learn a language. Also, one of the chief research professors who taught English as a Second Language said the same thing, but she didn't believe it.

Moreover, teaching English as a second language and teaching English through a series of grammar courses is death to literacy. I once had an English as a Second Language student ask whether I thought learning grammar was improving their language. I told her the truth. No, it doesn't, but the system has it all wrong. The system has been established to teach people with language deficiencies with grammar and not reading and writing.

I once made a presentation to my English colleagues about teaching grammar in the context of writing, and it was like I was talking to the wall. They could not relate to teaching grammar in that manner. I was teaching the proper use of mechanics, the correct word in a sentence, and sentence structure. The "lesson" wasn't very successful because they could not see themselves doing such a thing. I should have lectured them on the uselessness of teaching grammar in isolation of writing. They might have been offended. The issue is that teaching grammar has become so entrenched in the English canon that it might never be eradicated.

While teaching at the junior high school in those early days, I sensed that teaching grammar had little to do with improving writing, but I was guessing during those years. I did not see the need to teach grammar in isolation from writing. I needed to know how grammar knowledge translated to writing students. I felt that grammar needed to be incorporated into the teaching of writing. I tell the reader that teaching grammar with the writing is so much more gratifying than teaching it in isolation from the writing. For example, an essay with errors to be corrected can be distributed to the students, and with that focus in mind, students search for the mistakes until one is identified, and then the grammar teaching begins.

English teachers must learn how to incorporate grammar teaching into writing. Students should learn grammar during the process phase when

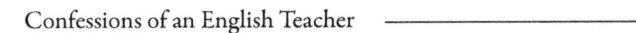

revising their writing. Students will learn grammar, mechanics, and usage differently, and success will be apparent over time with one revision after another.

Chapter 9:
Great English Departments Organize the Teaching of Usage

The actress Jodie Foster had issues working with Generation Z and saying they were annoying. Another complaint was about their writing: "Like, in emails, I'll tell them this is all grammatically incorrect, did you not check your spelling?" (BBC News January 2024 by Charlotte Gallager "Jodie Foster: Gen Z can be 'really annoying' to work with.") I believe she was referring to the misuse of language, not just spelling issues. The misuse of language is a problem with usage. A usage problem is put under the umbrella of grammar problems by most people who do not distinguish grammar from usage since the two are different. The irony is that English teachers rarely teach usage and do not distinguish it from grammar teaching. Therefore, the two are often lumped together whenever the older generations complain about the misuse of grammar by the younger generations. I wish to argue that those who see our current generations as incapable of articulating their language don't have grammar issues so much as they have usage issues. Perhaps examining why they exist will shed light on how students appear illiterate.

First, English teachers teach usage less than they teach grammar. Again, there is the misguided notion that teaching grammar is the grand approach to improving writing. We know that this is not true. If one looks at a grammar book, there are chapters and chapters of grammar lessons and no chapters devoted to teaching usage. H. Ramsey Fowler's *The Little, Brown Handbook* is one of the best grammar books ever. However, the usage part of the book is in the back, and it is identified as the "Glossary of Usage." In other words, essential usage words and phrases are listed in the book almost as an afterthought. Ironically, this "Glossary of Usage" is a compendium of words and phrases that most students make mistakes in their writing. For example, how often does one see the misuse of "there," "their," and "they're"? Perhaps one of the most abused sets of words in the English language.

Another cause of the misuse of language is that usage is not taught because there are no "lessons" associated with teaching it. Instead of making lessons to teach students to use words often misused in the English language correctly, the author made a glossary of those crucial words. A glossary isn't sufficient to teach students to use them correctly in their writing. Some organized lessons on using these words will help students better understand their usage in writing. An English teacher should also review common usage mistakes when revising the writing. In short, I advocate teaching these usage terms; I prefer that they be taught in the context of the student's writing. For example, after completing a second rough draft, students can check their writing to use the three "there's" properly. Teaching the students to use those words properly in their writing will solidify their understanding of their, there, and they're.

English teachers can organize the teaching of usage for the four years of high school (although it can start earlier). A review of the more important uses of commonly misused words can be discussed. There are practices that students can perform with the words. Learning the vast majority of commonly misused words will be an ongoing practice for several years, and students will know the correct use of those terms at the end of their high school years. English teachers will also reinforce using these terms in the students' writing.

I often told my students that a grammar book is a reference book. They should access the *Little, Brown Handbook* if they want some clarification about the proper usage or whether their grammar is being used correctly. Because my colleagues knew nothing about the "practice" of teaching grammar in the context of a piece of writing, all of my efforts to try and introduce them to do so were brushed aside. Breaking down the traditions of teaching English is a challenging change for Education, like any change when a new approach is discovered.

Chapter 10:
Great English Departments Know
What Writings Colleges Require

I was teaching at a high school for about fifteen years when one of the positions in the senior English group of teachers came about because of a retirement. The English Department grouped teachers on the class level they taught that year. In other words, the department has freshman and sophomore teachers and junior and senior teachers. I was asked to join the senior teachers because of the retirement opening. I was only vaguely aware of what they were teaching at that level then, but I was soon introduced to the curriculum. It was sometime in the 1990s, and composition had become a topic discussed at conferences and the establishment of writing centers nationwide. I had already taken multiple courses at the University of California at Irvine to enhance my ability to teach writing. As with anything new to the educational realm, the teaching of writing took off when the National Writing Project was established in 1974. State Centers like the California Writing Project for teaching writing were established in the decades following the beginning of the national writing project.

When I sat down in the new group, there were three women, and I was replacing a woman. I am not being sexist in writing such a statement because it is germane to what happens. The group had become good friends, and they all trusted each other's judgments about what they called the senior project or the senior term paper. These English teachers had created a project requiring their students to spend an entire semester writing this paper. The paper required the students to compare two poems from a gigantic list of British or American poets. I kept my thoughts to myself during the meeting and had to accept the paper if I wanted to teach senior English. At the time, I was unaware that they had exercised this paper on students for ten years. I listened to them talk about the importance of the paper and the time they would spend on it. I was appalled when it was discussed that the paper would take an entire semester. I could not grasp such an endeavor. I wondered where they learned to do such a thing in their English teacher training. I am confident that none spent an entire semester on a single writing.

The next day, the first senior students came into the classroom sullen and downtrodden. I had known many of them from teaching sophomore and junior English, so it was easy for them to open up about their feelings. Several asked, "Do we have to write the senior poetry paper, or can we do something else?" The paper had a reputation passed on to the next class through the rumor mill, and the words used to describe how they felt about it were not good. So, for my three periods of senior English, discussion ensued about getting around doing that paper. They must have sensed I had already judged the paper as unworthy. But I had to put my foot down and say they had to do it because I could not unilaterally change the paper.

Teaching the paper was the most miserable, gut-wrenching semester I had done in my twenty years of teaching English. It was pathetic because the paper was fraught with several problems. I did not like the paper because it did not "transfer" to the next level of learning: college. It was so useless I could not tell the reader how miserable it made the students and myself trying to pass this writing off as something significant. The writing aimed to compare the poetic devices of the two poems and show their similarities and differences. Creating a paper like this could only come from the minds of English teachers trained to think about literary terminology. I guess the paper's goal was to teach students the poetry terminology. English teachers are built to think like this. Instead of analyzing the poems, the students compared the poetic devices of the two poems. Instead of interpretation, students were bogged down in defining metonymy, personification, and other poetic devices. No college English department ever requires writing about poetic devices, which illustrates the gap between what high schools assign and what is done at the college level.

The senior English teachers proposed that the paper have a thesis. In my next meeting with them, I asked the group what the paper's thesis was supposed to be. They said that it was a statement that compared the two poems. Does that qualify as a thesis? A thesis is a claim that needs to be supported by evidence. No claims were being made in this paper. How can I teach a thesis when there is none? It was simply an expository comparison-contrast paper.

At the time of this paper, I had taught freshman composition in college for about seventeen years at various community colleges. The community colleges were mandated to teach about six or seven compositions, and the research paper was a Modern Language Association-style writing that dealt with a controversial subject. The MLA-style research paper had to be eight to ten pages long with a minimum of five sources. It seemed logical for seniors to write a paper of this nature using the same style to prepare them for their college composition class. After all, aren't the high school English classes College Prep courses? At the end of the semester, the seniors all managed to finish the project, and I made it as easy on them as possible. Despite this, these kids were angry that they had to do such a ridiculous paper. They did not care for an intense study of poetry.

English teachers think learning the literary devices associated with a kind of literature is essential. The irony is that none of them knew about literature that way. As English majors, we read and discussed literary works but only spent a little time on literary terminology. We studied and wrote about literature, but literary terminology was separate from the English major's work. So, the question became why they were doing this kind of writing. My first thought is that English teachers don't know squat about how to teach writing, especially about literature. English majors are not taught how to teach writing of any kind during the so-called "training" to be an English teacher. So, can it be that they don't know what writing to teach? Are they teaching this writing to prepare students for a standardized test? What is the goal of the writing? Under what circumstances are students' poetic knowledge measured? The California state tests? I read those tests, and they were awful. The standardized tests did not measure what we were teaching in class, and certainly, there were not a lot of questions about literary terminology. The standardized tests measured things like word use in a sentence, some grammatical knowledge, and many questions about rhetoric. No one taught rhetoric.

At the beginning of the following year, I announced that I would not teach the senior project paper and would be doing my version of a senior paper. We sat in the classroom with the English Department chair and in groups, and he overheard my announcement. The group asked me why I wasn't going to do the paper. I then bluntly told them that the paper was inappropriate for students' preparation for college and that the students hated doing the paper, and it was not what we, as English teachers, are here to do. We are not here to make students hate English. One of the English teachers started bawling her eyes out like I was murdering someone in the classroom (as opposed to in the cathedral) and started wailing like a stuck pig. The department chair came running over to the group and told me I had to do the paper or else! I told him I had the academic freedom to teach what I felt was important for students and thought our paper was nonsense. The other two English teachers in the group just sat stunned. It was total turmoil. It was a bombshell to try to go against city hall. When I think back on it after many years, it was an effort to upset the apple cart of tradition in teaching English. English teachers always believe that the writing students must do must be literary. This isn't the case. They need a wide variety of writings.

The English department chair ran to the front office for a quick meeting with the principal, like a child taking his basketball, going home, and leaving all the players without one on the basketball court. He looked at me before he left the room and said with his look, I'll teach you. So our meeting ended, and the two women who weren't crying were consoling the one who was. I left the room and went back to my room. I waited for the phone call and prepared my thoughts for the eventual meeting with the principal. It was only a short time before I was "called on the carpet," so to speak, and was asked to report to the principal's office. I did so immediately because I had an explanation as to why our English Department was teaching the wrong paper. These English teachers did not know what they were doing when teaching a piece of writing. They were not looking forward to the challenges students faced in college. If their program is a college prep program, they need to investigate what writings would best prepare students for college classes. They did not do that, so English departments need to look forward to the writing students will do in college and investigate what they will be. These teachers did not do that.

He was waiting for me when I got to the principal's office. He was friendly, but what did he know about teaching English? I recalled that he once taught science before he hated teaching and moved into administration. He was fair and asked me to explain why I wanted to change how the senior English paper was taught since those learning it had been doing it that way for the last ten years. I did not know how long they had been teaching the paper, and I was shocked when I learned that. It was a Shirley Jackson "Lottery" moment. The English department chair had told the principal, and he was armed with that information. My first response was that I didn't know this group of teachers had been punishing students for that long. I then asked if I could explain where I was coming from. The principal may be receptive to a different paper for students than the current one the senior English teachers created.

I told the principal that most of the students from our high school would be going to community colleges because most of them were not academic, and most could not afford to go elsewhere anyway. I then indicated that I had taught at those community colleges for fifteen years and knew the kinds of papers the students would be required to write. It seemed logical to prepare those students for the next level of instruction by ensuring they could write an MLA (Modern Language Association) style research paper. I then indicated that the paper would be argumentative to improve the student's ability to do critical thinking. Critical thinking was at an all-time high buzzwords then, and I knew that part of the principal's goal for that year was to encourage teachers to teach critical thinking. I then gave him several examples of subjects students could write about in the paper. I showed him papers written by college students that demonstrated what I wanted our seniors to do. He sat back and listened to me for about half an hour.

At the end of the presentation, he agreed to allow me to teach my paper to my students, stipulating that I would also teach the other members of the English department how to teach the paper. He asked that I be prepared to teach them the following year and allow the teaching of the current paper for another year. I agreed to comply, and we shook hands. I went back to my classroom but stopped in the room where the meeting had taken place. The department chair was there consoling the three teachers, and I looked in and said, "You get one more year with this paper, and then mine is implemented next year." I then went to my room to prepare to teach the ugly paper one more year, but I was elated that things would change at this high school for the good. Students would go to community colleges or four-year colleges ready to write the MLA-style research paper.

When I finally got the other department members to recognize the need for an argumentative paper, I needed to start teaching the other teachers what an argumentative thesis was. I xeroxed portions of my college text so they could learn what an argumentative thesis is supposed to sound like. It took a while for some of them to get the hang of it, but over time, they understood that a paper with a controversial issue had a thesis and that arguing required research to back up the arguments. The teachers found a way to use research effectively to teach the research paper. Students began learning to use MLA style, and many of them graduating were confident that they could write their papers at the college level without having the learning curve of what it takes to write an MLA-style research paper. The whole point of this has been to illustrate that English teachers arrive at the secondary level not prepared to teach any writing other than literary writing.

I taught hundreds of seniors my paper for another fifteen or so years. It was extraordinarily successful, preparing students to write the MLA-style research paper in freshman English and all the community colleges in Orange County, California. Even though this is precisely the type of paper that Common Core requires, the current English Department at my former school no longer teaches it. The ignorance of the teaching of writing to prepare students for college continues.

Chapter 11:
Great English Departments Teach Essays for the College-Bound

Writing improves when taught how to develop writing through the writing process and shown how to do it. Writing randomly does not improve writing. Teaching students how to structure a literary paper is teaching writing. As an English instructor at the community college, I led the students through the literary paper instead of assigning it. I taught the paper and what a literary paper is supposed to be. Teaching a scholarly paper is essential for several reasons.

For the most part, a college education will include writing about literature and being prepared to do so will increase the success rate of students. For my first-year college composition class, we read *The Catcher in the Rye* and wrote an analysis of it. I taught students that reading literature is concluding what is read, and those conclusions become the basis for the paper. One of those conclusions is the thesis of the paper. From there, the students were taught how to support the thesis from the evidence in the book. I did not do what my high school English teachers and college professors did to us. They assigned a literary analysis of *Hamlet* and asked us to submit it in three weeks—no direction, suggestions, organization, outline, or anything. In my view, that was just ridiculous teaching. Since literature professors were not writing teachers, they could not offer suggestions about how to write the paper. Of all my English professors, only one professor told us how to structure our essays for the mid-term and final exams. Other than that, we had to learn how to write our papers independently. Then, some of them were indignant when we failed.

We write about literature to deepen our understanding of the social history that it represents. Literature has a time and a place. This setting comes at a historical time when students must understand what the author intended with the work. Writing literary papers deepens our understanding of those times and places in which the writing takes place. Novels and plays are works of literature that engender the scholarly essays we write. We learn about the social time and place of the novel or play, improving our understanding of those who lived in that period and their struggles. Harper Lee's *To Kill a Mockingbird* is a literary work transforming us into a time and place most students might never experience. We learn of the prejudice of the Southern people about the black man. We know of the tragedy of Tom Robinson. It was not the best of times for black people in the South in the 1940s and for a very long time before and after that. The novel allows us to relive that time and gain a perspective on what has happened historically to those people we come to know in the novel. We write literary papers to learn empathy. Literature is the foundation upon which students are asked to improve their literacy. Writing about the literature that they read is how literacy develops. Interpreting a character's behavior in a book can be the basis for writing. The interpretation of the reading is a different story.

Students do not bring their literary skills to interpret literature and find interpretation difficult. It is difficult for English teachers to be as skilled at teaching the understanding of literature without a master's degree. Writing about literature is challenging, and there are better books than Edgar V. Roberts's book *Writing About Literature* to teach students to write about literature. I used an early version of the book in my average classes, and the reading needed to be more straightforward for the average student.

When I lived in Irvine for the first year or so, I lived next door to a French professor who taught at the University of California at Irvine. He was a scholar of Montaigne and a wonderfully funny man. We ran together when I lived near him, but his knew went bad, and he had to forgo running. He took up cycling, and I joined him until I was nearly wiped out on the Orange County roads by a hapless driver. He continued to ride his bike as long as I knew him. When we ran together, we discussed poetry and the interpretation of it using deconstruction. He once told me that reading becomes writing and that writing fosters another writing. If we are to improve our students' writing, it is best to use reading to foster their writing.

Chapter 12:
Great English Departments Have Writing Labs

Writing labs are essential to an English department and should be a staple that students can rely upon to improve the writing they are required to do. They are also essential for students who need access to a computer word-processing program they do not have at home. The existence of the writing lab will help students in several ways.

Students are more likely to exercise the writing process if they can rewrite papers several times before final submission. Rewriting improves writing, and teaching students to rewrite to improve a paper is very important. Any piece of good writing has several drafts before the final writing is submitted to the teacher or the publisher. A writing lab will help facilitate that process. A writing lab allows students to write several drafts of a paper, whereas putting pen to paper is less likely to be done.

Writing labs are helpful to students who cannot afford a laptop or a desktop computer. Since most teachers are unaware of a student's economic status, it is essential to provide that service so the economically deprived student can complete the work as requested. Writing lab availability is an important issue, and ideally, it can be set up near the library where the assistant librarian can monitor its use. Placing a writing lab without a monitor is a total waste of the use of a writing lab. A writing lab should be available before, during, and after school. The staff can arrange scheduled visits by classes with those teachers willing to bring a whole class to the library.

If the word processing programs use Grammarly, students can learn a lot of grammar. Grammarly will help students modify their sentences so they can see the benefit of change. Grammarly will likely have better sentence constructions and help teach them grammar. Programs that improve students' writing will also help them learn spelling, mechanics, and proper usage. A writing lab with good word processing programs does that.

Learning to exercise the writing process is a massive benefit of a writing lab. Students can go through the process of creating a draft, getting feedback from an instructor or other students, and rewriting the original. As students continue to rewrite their drafts, they will learn the importance of revision, the heart of writing. Rewritten essays are more likely to be better products than rough drafts, and improved writing will result from learning the importance of writing and rewriting.

The writing lab is vital to a good education, and students who do not have computers at home are disadvantaged. All community colleges and colleges have writing labs where students can get assistance and feedback on their writing. The secondary school is a good training ground for using a writing lab for students going on to college, but they don't exist in as many high schools as they should.

Part C:
Hallmarks of a Literature Program

Chapter 13:
Great English Departments Have a Well-Organized Literature and Nonfiction Reading Program

I have sometimes dreamt, at least, that when the Day of Judgment dawns and the great conquerors and lawyers and statesmen come to receive their rewards— their crowns, their laurels, their names carved indelibly upon imperishable marble—the Almighty will turn to Peter. It will say, not without particular envy, when he sees us coming with our books under our arms, "Look, these need no reward. We have nothing to give them here. They love reading."

—Virginia Woolf, "How Should One Read a Book?"

I used to be able to list all thirty-two works of literature that we were required to read from our freshman year to our senior year in high school from 1962-1966. We were to do these readings outside of class for each year of English. My freshman year reading consisted of *Ivanhoe* by Sir Walter Scott, *Animal Farm* by George Orwell, *The Pearl* by John Steinbeck, *The*

Iliad and *The Odyssey* by Homer, *The Diary of a Young Girl* by Anne Frank, and *Romeo and Juliet* by William Shakespeare. The sophomore, junior, and senior years were followed by at least eight classics each year. In short, we were overwhelmed with the reading of literature. The argument was that literature elevates our language, so we read it to increase our operating language. Whether reading, writing, or speaking vocabulary, literature was the tool to get us there. All of these works were our responsibility. We had to read the books and be prepared to write about them or discuss them when the time had elapsed. We took tests on the books. We swam in literature. Nearly sixty years later, in the state of California, the reading of literature still dominates the classroom. I suppose literature is going to continue to dominate the English classes in the state of California. In that case, there should be an effort to adjust the literature to the reading ability level of the students at the schools.

We became English teachers because we loved reading literature. We loved books, plays, and poetry. We like reading the story and the world the story created. The literature program for the English department should be established and prepared for each level of student and then for each grade level of student. English classes are essentially "dictated" by the state of California because of the books one has to use to teach English. Publishing companies design the books for each state to reflect their wishes. States like Texas have input on what the textbooks can and cannot say. English textbooks in California are literature books. The first- and second-year student books are designed around four different genres: short stories, poetry, novels, and plays—the first two years of high school English center around teaching these four genres and their literary terminology.

In the first quarter of the year, students will read short stories, discuss the stories, and write about them. A heavy emphasis is placed on teaching the genre terminology of the short story: character, plot, setting, symbol, irony, and several other terms associated with the short story. The second quarter consists of teaching poetry and the associated terminology of poetry. Metaphors, similes, stanzas, rhymes, and several other poetic terms are taught in association with the poems read in the book. High school students are students of literature. English teachers are like little professors pontificating about literature. English teachers attempt to teach the analysis of literature by teaching its terminology. It fails miserably. The third and fourth quarters are repeated with the novel, the play, and associated terminology. This structure is what a school year consists of for the first two years of English.

The third and fourth years of English are a survey of American and English literature. These courses are taught chronologically from the beginning of literature in America to the contemporary era. The teaching of British literature in the senior year is done similarly. Knowing that English teachers are "forced" to teach English in this manner creates issues with teaching English. Teaching American literature and British literature dominates the coursework for English. The books are so long and involve teaching everything in them, which is easily the work of three semesters of English. So, there is a great deal that isn't taught. Both of these literature surveys should be required for college freshmen or sophomores.

If the assigned textbooks are mandatory reading for students, then a discretionary approach must be taken when deciding what should and should not be taught. Literature can be untenable for average students. For honors students, an English teacher can throw anything at them, and they will read it and regurgitate it back to the one who delivered it. Therefore, structuring a literature program for students can be difficult, and the following must be kept in mind.

What is the ethnicity of the literature audience? Literature that is taught to students should be something that they can identify with. Long-held notions that certain books need to be taught are flat-out wrong. Some novels fit more suitably to the audience of students who are different ethnically than in the past. New literature needs a fresh place in the teaching world of English. If there are students of color, then literature adjustments to the program must address those concerns by reading works for that endeavor.

Another feature of a well-adjusted literature program is knowing the readability of the literature students read and ensuring that reading is accomplishable instead of dreadful. What is the purpose of literature that is too far above the students' reading level? From reading literature beyond their linguistic reach. Literature should be chosen for its readability, entertainment value, and relevance to the students.

Common Core's new standards emphasize teaching less literature than ever. Under Common Core, students are to read a great deal more nonfiction. If the new textbooks have not incorporated nonfiction works, then it is necessary to find those works to adjust the reading program to reflect less literature and more nonfiction reading. The teaching of literature is no longer the primary focus of the English class. There is a new emphasis on "informational literacy." It is about time that teaching English allows students to explore topics other than those in the world of fiction. Great English departments are making these adjustments to their programs.

There are still some entertaining readings for English teachers: *How to Read Literature Like a Professor: A Lively and Entertaining Guide to Reading Between the Lines* by Thomas C. Foster and *Teaching Literature Rhetorically* by Jennifer Fletcher.

Part D:
English Department Hallmarks

Chapter 14:
Great English Departments Provide Course Descriptions, Course Outlines, and Lesson Plans for All Regular Courses

One day during prep week, I was organizing the English Department book rooms, where novels and textbooks of various sorts were sorted and checked out to teachers. A new teacher entered the room and asked me where the novels for *Huckleberry Finn* were. I showed her where they were but had to ask why she would be interested in that novel. "I'm going to teach it," she said. "Now?" I asked, and she replied, "Yes." I decided it was a mentor-teacher moment. I explained to the young lady that junior English American literature should be taught chronologically. I told her it was what the California English Language Arts Standards for public schools mandate. This is pre-Common Core, but if the junior year is to teach American literature, then teaching it chronologically is an introduction to the writers of our culture.

Chronological order means that one had to teach the course from the beginning of the Colonial Period of American literature and move through the different eras of literature to the Modern and Postmodern eras. As I indicated to the new teacher, it is time to teach *Huckleberry Finn* when one reaches the age of realism. The young lady then asked me why no one had told her that. I told her I would assume that the other teachers would have indicated that to her when she was in her junior-level meetings. She told me the other teachers said teaching the course was her choice. It was an instance that reflected the rogue ways in which English teachers at that school approached teaching English. English teachers are permitted to teach however they feel like it.

There were many instances of this behavior at my high school, where I taught most of my teaching years. Some junior English teachers spent the entire first quarter teaching *The Crucible* by Arthur Miller. Some English teachers spent a whole semester teaching *Hamlet*. Some teachers taught whatever they wanted without accountability for that behavior. If the state standards at the time were to teach American and English literature chronologically, then we should all abide by that requirement. The idea was to expose our students to the literature of England and America. Doing so is just part of becoming educated. We had a giant textbook to teach, and the book was organized chronologically, not by genre. Is this the best way to teach this literature? Perhaps not. They could be taught thematically. They should be taught by genre. If Common Core demands an equal representation of non-fiction and fictional readings, then a genre approach might best teach these two subjects. Chronological order cannot make sense if Common Core demands equality of nonfiction with fiction.

I told the young lady to start reading the literature from the text-book for the Colonial Period, and I would provide her with all the lessons for teaching that unit. I also gave her the final test for the unit. She had to prepare the colonial literature in the textbook and do the assignments as I had designed. She was eternally grateful. She followed my teaching of American literature for the remainder of the year. When we got to the re-alistic era, she taught *Huckleberry Finn* using the lesson plans I had devised for the regular students over many years. She couldn't believe the work that I had created. I told her that the curriculum for a course is developed over time and is partially created the first time one teaches a piece of literature.

After this encounter, I decided that all English teachers should have an outline of the course and the lesson plans handed to them when they arrive at the school to teach. This is one of the hallmarks of a great English department. This approach existed at Fullerton High School, and it worked beautifully. New English teachers are overwhelmed by the chal-lenge of teaching English, so presenting them with lesson plans and tests will allow them to instruct students immediately. With a course outline and lesson plans included, new English teachers "hit the ground running" with their students and did not have to "burn the midnight oil" building a cur-riculum for a required course that should already be created. Why reinvent the wheel?

It isn't beneficial to students to have a new teacher fumbling around trying to figure out what to do. Students immediately benefit from a "pre-pared" English teacher. Students are immediately getting the instruction they deserve despite having a new teacher.

With these prepared lesson plans, the new teacher will have time to read the works to be taught. With a good foundation for teaching the course, the high stress of teaching English is considerably diminished. Students will become more engaged because the new teacher is prepared with lessons. With the tests in hand, the new teacher can direct the teaching to the test, knowing the material that needs to be covered. The new teacher can even improve on the materials handed to them if they wish.

Course outlines are beneficial to the student and the teacher. A course outline is a guideline for the student and the teacher because it lays out a "plan" for what the course will cover and what the students can expect to learn. English teachers who "fly by the seat of their pants" are terrible English teachers. Not having a structure for what is taught means denying the student an education. I often cringed when I learned that English teachers took an entire semester to teach one play or research paper! Some English teachers would spend ten weeks on one novel! English teachers who perform such teaching demonstrate that they are going rogue and doing what they think is right for them and not for their students. They do not have a structure, and although they have a mandate to teach the course requirements, they only teach what they wish and how long they teach the literature.

A course outline is a contract, and the contract is something that both sides need to fulfill. The English teacher needs to cover the course material, and the students need to learn the course material. It should not be an English teacher's prerogative to ignore the course material and "dance to the beat of their drum." Why did English teachers not learn this in their college classes? Course outlines are a staple in a college class. Students know what to expect when they see a course outline. A course in Shakespeare covered a certain amount of material, and the professor covered that material. The professor did not decide to teach one play for ten weeks of the semester as English teachers at the high school level are prone to do. It is shameful what English teachers get away with—teaching *Hamlet* for an entire semester is incredibly ludicrous. The English teacher needs to prepare the material outlined in the course outline and fulfill the "contract" they have with students, and the students need to learn the material that the English teachers cover. Almost everything a student learns in high school is background material (schema) that they will need for college. I could not imagine not covering as much material as possible for my honors students, who were so willing to learn anything and everything I could teach them so they were prepared for their studies at the college level. Isn't this what a college-bound curriculum is supposed to be?

Lesson plans also need to be created for the new English teacher. Those plans are essential for Common Core since these standards will be new to the first-time English teacher. Designing lesson plans that keep with the standards helps create a paper trail for preparing students for the standardized test administered to measure Common Core achievements. The new English teachers are overwhelmed by the curriculum preparation required to teach one class, much less the preparation necessary for two and sometimes three courses. New English teachers need lesson plans so they can use the time to focus on reading the materials for the class instead of creating the curriculum. Doing so will allow the new teacher to get off to a good start teaching their classes. It will also allow their students to get off to a good learning start.

At Fullerton High School, I taught in the reading and English departments. When I arrived in the English department, the chair introduced me to the file cabinets where all the course outlines and lesson plans for the courses taught in the English department for the regular students were. They did not have them for the honors or AP English classes. However, they had course outlines, lesson plans, and tests for all the other courses in the English department.

Preparing the materials for new teachers can be done as a group project for those who teach the same grade. Developing the appropriate materials for the new teacher would take little time, given that veteran teachers already have good lesson plans. An English department must think as a group instead of rogue individuals who work at their own pace and forget that educating the students and developing their literacy is their responsibility. Teaching one piece of literature for an entire semester is not a reasonable way to improve students' literacy. Students need exposure to many different works of literature.

Chapter 15:
Great English Departments Establish an Assessment Program

English teachers do not assess their student's skills at the beginning of the year, at the end of the semester, or at the end of the year. Teachers who have earned a master's degree in reading do. Reading teachers are taught to test their student's abilities at the beginning and the end of the semester and complete a post-evaluation at the end of the year. When I became a reading teacher at Fullerton High School, I learned to evaluate the reading gains that my students made over each semester. Writing gains can also be measured, and language skills are measurable. Reading gains are measurable, and so is one's cultural literacy. Great English departments will likely do this. Measuring the gains illustrates that teaching has happened and student growth is occurring. English departments must rely on something other than the mandated Common Core standardized tests, which have already been demonstrated as total failures.

The Nelson Reading Test, the Nelson-Denny Reading Test, or The California Test of Basic Skills can measure a student's reading gains. These tests are not administered because most English teachers need to learn about them. All of these tests measure the vocabulary and comprehension levels of the students. The tests also determine a grade level equivalent. For example, students who take the vocabulary test arrive at a score of twenty-five, and this number is equivalent to a reading grade level score of 9.6. The 9.6 means that the student is reading at the ninth-grade level and six months into the next level, the tenth grade. In other words, the student is nearly reading at the tenth-grade level. Measuring the vocabulary level is a way of determining how effective the vocabulary programs that English teachers use in their classes are. The test also measures the student's reading comprehension level. Improvement in the ability to comprehend what one is reading is an essential indicator of the success of the teaching.

Assessing the students is essential to the teacher of English because the students can be guided to books that are just above their measured reading level. Good assessment tools mean teachers can better assign reading for the Independent Reading Program. Students who read books just above their reading level will likely gain literacy more quickly than those who read materials too far above their current reading level. This is a controversial subject because professors of English would argue that the literature level does not matter. It does not matter for them, but it does for the student who needs to bring a larger vocabulary to the reading. It is essential to realize that what a student brings to the reading is more important than the reading itself. A student who brings vocabulary two or more grade levels below the book's reading level will not have a good "conversation" with that book. It's as simple as that.

Aside from evaluating their reading abilities, English teachers can measure their writing with prewriting at the beginning and the end of the semester. A rubric score can be assigned to the pretest, and the same rubric can be used to measure the posttest. Measuring the growth of student writing is another way to demonstrate that English teachers are showing growth to the public and especially to the parents of their students. It is a way to ward off criticism from those who use the Common Core Standardized Test to punish teachers for their apparent ineptitude. Therefore, English departments can illustrate their performance as a group with writing scores that demonstrate the writing growth of their students.

Ironically, English teachers do not measure their students' writing improvement. Again, this is a failure on the part of the education program that teachers get "trained" to teach English. In my entire career, it was never discussed as an option for teachers in the classroom, even though I brought up the subject numerous times. I asked, "How do we know if our students' writing is improving if we don't measure the growth of the writing from the beginning to the end of the year? I measured the students' skills in every college class I taught by asking them to draft a thesis and argue a position on any topic they chose. When students arrived at the end of the semester, I gave them the same option to perform writing on a topic of their choice. The difference in performance was measured by a rubric score given to the writing. The pretest was measured with the rubric, and the same rubric was used on the posttest to measure the students' writing. The scores improved dramatically because the students wrote six essays during the semester and a research paper toward the end of the semester. They handled the posttest a lot better than the pretest.

English skills can also be measured. I firmly believe that what the public perceives as the inability of English teachers to teach "grammar" is the misinterpretation of usage as grammar. When students make the mistake of misusing "fewer" and "less," they are making a usage mistake. There are many usage mistakes, and because usage is randomly taught if taught at all, we find our students making these mistakes in their writing and while speaking. These usage errors can be remediated with good teaching during the writing process. Students can be taught how to use "their," "they're," and "there" when their writings are given feedback. Grammar skills can also be measured as long as students are taught the grammar in the context of their writing and not in isolation. These skills can be measured with a criterion-referenced test that the instructor devises to measure the skills taught. A group criterion-referenced test can be designed if the department is in sync.

Another measure of student growth can be the language skills of the students. A basic grammar, usage, and mechanics test can be established to measure the student's knowledge at the beginning of the semester. The teacher would devise the test to measure the skills the students will learn each semester. As I have already indicated, if grammar is taught, it should be taught in the context of teaching writing and proper usage. If students are taught "there," "they're," and "their" in the writing they are doing, the learning is more likely to be permanent. Also, if a student has used an active verb in their writing, then teaching the adverb to modify it is the best way to teach grammar. Students will learn grammar if taught in the context of discussing writing they have done. This can be done during a conference with the student when feedback is given. Grammar is internalized with reading as well.

The literary skills of the students can also be measured since English teachers place so much emphasis on teaching literary language. Literary terminology is the language of literature, and knowing what a metaphor and a simile are is part of that learning. The language of poetry is important and should be learned. The language of fiction and nonfiction should be part of the terminology study of students. It is the knowledge they will need in college. Measuring their understanding of these terms can be done quarterly if the English teacher teaches a genre per quarter in the first two years of high school. Again, this is considered a criterion-referenced test created by the instructor to measure the learning taught in the classroom over time. Measuring students' skills with a standardized test like Common Core is an absolute joke. It does not measure a student's performance in the classroom, and a test like that is heavily biased in favor of high-achieving students.

English teachers can measure the reading skills, writing and language skills, and literary terminology to demonstrate the learning students have done over a semester or for the entire year. Establishing an assessment program of skills that students are to learn in an English class demonstrates the accountability of the teachers, reflects the learning that students have done, and it proves to the public that learning is taking place. This is the antidote to the insanity of Common Core, a standardized test designed to make students fail. Common Core is an effort to show that public schools cannot successfully teach students when we all know that is just hogwash. English teachers can be their own advocates by assessing students' classroom learning compared to standardized testing.

Chapter 16:
Great English Departments Need a Leader with a Master's Degree in English, Composition, or Reading

As I indicated in my memoir, the English department chair should have excellent credentials to lead the largest group of academic teachers on campus. The chair should know the State Standards for Language Arts that must be taught in the classroom. The chair should also possess a master's degree in English or a related subject. The chair should demonstrate knowledge of the English and reading curriculum in front of the English department members. Let's look deeper at the characteristics of a great English department head.

The English department chair must have a master's in reading, composition, or literature. In short, that person should know the curriculum and be able to mentor all teachers in the department. The English department head is the leader of the curriculum of that department. The department chair should lead the presentations to the department. English department chairs should be able to understand the issues confronting English teachers. A good curricular program can only be established with good leadership. Leadership requires the knowledge necessary to improve the overall program. Without it, the overall program will suffer, with the students being the losers. An English department chair is a curriculum leader for the English teachers in the department.

The English department chair is the curriculum leader who organizes with his teachers what will be taught in each class. The English department chair should show leadership in setting up the course descriptions for the counseling department, the course outlines for the courses taught in the department, and the general lesson plans for the course. All of this can be accomplished with the help of his English department. The department chair should be aware of the curriculum taught in each of the four levels of English taught in the department. Leading the English teachers in creating these materials would allow new English teachers to begin teaching right from the start of their assignments.

The chair must be a curriculum leader who is aware of the current trends in the teaching of English. For example, the English department chair should lead the discussion about teaching writing as a process. If the English department chair isn't aware of teaching writing as a process, they should not be the English department chair. If the English department chair is unaware of a rubric, they should not be the department chair. In short, whatever is trending in teaching English should be something the department chair shares with the teachers.

The English department chair should lead the discussion about all curriculum concerns in the department. If the department chair knows the subject well, it is important to lead discussions on subjects related to the teaching of English. If there are essential kinds of essays that students need to write for their classes, then the department chair should lead the discussion on that subject. If the English department chair is not aware of the trends in the teaching of English, then someone aware should replace them.

The department chair should be aware of the evaluation methods of writing. Using a rubric to evaluate students' writing should be a standard for essays required by the English department. Evaluation tools should be consistent so that students do not interpret the evaluation of writing as something haphazard. What do students think when confronted with various evaluation methods for their writing? It speaks volumes about the need for more professionalism in teaching English.

The English department chair should be aware of the teaching of writing using the writing process. Teaching students to write, receive feedback, and rewrite a paper is the basis of learning how to use the writing process while completing a paper. This important topic should be an ongoing topic of education for English teachers. Teaching students to revise a paper is an essential step in making students independent writers. When students learn how to write and revise a paper, they have been taught a vital strategy for presenting their best writing to their teachers.

Also, the history of teaching composition is certainly something the department chair should lead. If the department chair is aware of the language of rhetoric, then it is incumbent on the part of the English department chair to lead the discussion about how to accomplish this. Demonstrating a knowledge of the history of rhetoric is important to college-bound students and for understanding argumentation. The English department chair is aware of the language of rhetoric and teaches it to the English department.

The department chair reads and provides professional development opportunities and journals for teaching English to his department. Magazines like the *English Journal* and the *Reading Journal* are important to the development of the abilities of the English department staff. The department chair should be aware of the leadership role that the position demands. The chair also encourages additional education in all aspects of English. The department chair should create opportunities for his staff to grow in this area. Even though budgets have been reduced for sending teachers to conferences, there is always room for professional development.

The chair should create unity among the department members by conducting inspiring and educational department meetings. English department meetings can be organized around a topic of interest to the staff. A well-conducted department meeting would open the eyes to the teaching of any aspect of the English department curriculum.

The chair will choose honors instructors with master's degrees in an English program. English department chairs cannot allow uninformed teachers to teach honors students. It is a disservice to the honors students who deserve the best and brightest teachers in the department. Teachers who are educated about their subject are more important than friendly teachers. Honors students need to be educated, and a teacher with a master's degree will be more likely to accomplish that task. Assigning teachers who are friends of the department chair but cannot teach honors students is a disservice to the students.

Finally, the chair is responsible for hiring the best candidates for new teaching positions in the English department. The English department chair cannot hire nepotistically or cronyistically. The department chair should select the best candidate from those who have applied, diversify the department with a balance of men and women, and include minority teachers. The diversity of the student body requires diversity in the staff teaching them.

The English department leadership can positively or negatively impact the performance of both teachers and students. Someone without the requisite knowledge to lead the department affects the overall literacy development of students at the school. A well-qualified person must be the department chair of the most important department in the school.

Chapter 17:
Great English Departments Have Honors
Teachers with a Master's in English

Teachers of English without master's degrees in literature should never be considered to teach an honors or AP English class. It takes a master's degree in literature to effectively teach that level of student. An English teacher with a master's degree in literature is much more informed about the literature of any era than one without that degree. A master's degree is thirty more literature units about English and American authors. Someone without that degree will not be able to communicate information learned via earning that degree.

Without a master's degree in literature, some students will likely be more intelligent than the teacher. Some honors students might be as well-read and informed as the teacher. Placing an undereducated teacher in front of honors students discourages them because they know the difference between teachers who know what they are talking about and those who don't. Most of the time, honors students cannot do anything about who is placed in front of them, but the department chair should put someone who knows what they are talking about. In my experience, I have seen individuals placed in front of teachers who could not handle the pressure of teaching that level of student because they were uninformed. Even though the honors teacher is undereducated, honors students learn to keep their mouths shut because they want a good grade.

Honors teachers with a master's degree in literature are more likely to be informed about the literature and the author of that literature. This is important to the honors student. Honors students are more likely to go to significant four-year colleges, and the more informed they are, the more prepared they will be for college. Honors teachers should lecture about what they know of the literature and inform them as best they can about that literature. It should be a requirement that anyone who teaches the honors students have a master's degree in literature. Yet, that was not the case at the school where I taught, and many of those honors students opened up in my class and complained about the lack of performance of their honors teachers. The honors student will not compromise their grade in the class and complain to the teacher themselves, but they want to do so. They knew they were getting less than they deserved. They are powerless to do anything about it. Parents must learn if their teachers have that degree if they are honors or Advanced Placement instructors.

A teacher who has finished a master's degree in literature has written many more literary papers than a teacher with a bachelor's degree in literature. The more literary papers written will allow the teacher to know how to teach a literary paper. This will be important to the student who attends a four-year major college. Knowing how to draft a thesis from reading a work of literature is a significant step toward a good education. The honors teacher should know how to do this. Honors students should be able to effectively write literary papers and, more importantly, learn to construct a well-documented Modern Language Association writing.

There is no question about an English teacher possessing a master's degree in literature to teach honors students. If this is not carried out successfully, then it is a disservice to the highest-achieving students in the school.

Chapter 18:
Great English Departments Hire
the Best Candidates

An essential feature of a great English department is who they hire to teach. In my previous book, I indicated that I had applied for an English and reading position at a high school near my home. With a master's degree in both subjects and the job calling for abilities in both areas, I felt confident I could get the job. After submitting the papers for the position, I waited for an interview call. It never came. After moving into the district a few years later, I learned how teachers were hired. Many of the hires were nepotistic or cronyistic. In the Irvine Unified School District, it was impossible to be hired on one's merits but on who one knew and not what one knew. This practice of hiring friends would be a chronic problem that I perceived not only in the district that I lived in but also in the district where I taught. English departments should hire the best job candidates.

The public deserves the best teachers in front of their children. When a school or a department at the high school level (or any level for that matter) hires someone less qualified than another who has applied, it affects the quality of instruction in that department. At any given time, the best person who has applied for the position should be that teacher. This is vital to the quality of instruction for the students at that school. When a department does otherwise, they hire people inferior to those with better credentials who were not considered for the position.

When an English department does not search for the best candidate for teaching in the department, it diminishes the overall performance of the department. Instead of a friend being hired for the position, another candidate might have an outstanding resume to bring to the department. This choice would be beneficial to the students as well. Doesn't the public deserve the best candidate to teach at our public schools? Improving the performance of the English department is dependent on hiring new teachers who are the best of the lot during the interviewing process. There are better ways to improve the quality of the English department than hiring friends and family and former school graduates.

During my tenure at the last high school I taught at, several good hires were former students, but there were weak hires as well, solely because the candidate was a school graduate. This is not a healthy practice, and the program is diminished when the best candidate who applies for any given job is not hired. Equally as important is to keep a balance of male and female instructors. Teaching in an English department with a significant imbalance is unfair to students. The ethnicity of the student body is also a consideration in hiring a new teacher, yet this was always overlooked in favor of nepotism and cronyism. I can only count how often English teachers were employed in the department, with a fair interview conducted by the administration or the English department. It is a sad commentary on the unfair approach to hiring new teachers.

Part II:
Community College and
English Department Hallmarks

Introduction to Community College and English Department Recommendations

Community colleges have traditions that are more entrenched than high schools, and they are traditions that have hurt students for many decades. There are several things that community colleges can do to improve the instruction of English for students. Community college English departments can establish course outlines and lesson plans for part-time teachers. Community colleges can teach compositions that are beneficial for students transferring to a four-year college. Community college English departments can improve the teaching of composition by hiring more composition instructors instead of literature instructors. Community college English departments can also improve instruction by hiring more reading instructors to improve the language of incoming second-language students and linguistically deficient native readers. Community colleges can improve the overall teaching by hiring more full-time instructors and removing the plethora of part-time instructors. Community college administrators can improve overall instruction by hiring qualified instructors and preventing

the hiring of friends and relatives. All community colleges can improve the instruction of students by offering a reintroduction to college classes.

Community college English departments can improve their instruction by reevaluating the teaching of grammar in composition classes. They can also improve student placement by evaluating their writing instead of placing them based on a grammar test. Also, community colleges can improve student overall instruction by creating full reading departments with reading classes for students deficient in the English language.

I wish to examine these recommendations in more detail in the following chapters. Some of these troublesome traditions may be altered in the years to come.

Part A:
English Department Hallmarks

Chapter 1:
English Departments Should Establish Course Outlines and Lesson Plans for Part-Time Instructors

Community college English departments can better serve their students by preparing course outlines and lesson plans for new part-time teachers. This is vital to improving the performance of all part-time faculty. Several part-time faculty told me they did not know what they were doing with the teaching of writing. This was especially true of new part-time instructors at Pikes Peak Community College, but it was a problem with most of the community colleges where I taught. English departments at community colleges expect part-time instructors to be able to teach composition classes. Nothing can be further from the truth. The course material must be designed and submitted to the part-time faculty hired to teach composition courses. Almost one hundred percent of the time, part-time faculty are hired in the English department to teach composition classes, but are never helped when structuring the class for their students. Therefore, it is vitally important that a complete set of lessons and course outlines be prepared for these part-time faculty members of the English department. Let me explain why.

First, most, if not all, faculty hired to teach English part-time are being asked to teach composition or grammar courses. All English departments at the community colleges who hire part-time faculty do nothing for the new hires. Since most of those hired are not writing instructors but literature instructors, these part-time members need to gain an understanding of how to teach composition. So, it is important that those who do not have the preparation to teach a writing course be "trained" by the English department. The English department can create the course materials for the new part-time faculty and then review them with them as part of their "training" to teach the writing courses. This way, the new part-time faculty can teach their courses more effectively with that support. Although it would be ideal to hire writing instructors, most of those hired have a literature master's degree.

Secondly, a course outline gives the part-time faculty a "road map" for navigating the teaching of the new course. Part-time faculty will be able to start teaching the course right away because they have not spent inordinate amounts of time researching how to teach the class. Oftentimes part-time faculty are hired to teach the course, but are only told what the book(s) are for the course, but given no direction about how to teach the class. I suggest that these preparations for the course are entirely the responsibility of the full-time faculty. It would be easy to generate the course materials for part-time instructors. The materials necessary to teach the course can be prepared for the new part-time faculty.

Most importantly, students who take part-time instructors for classes will be cheated from good instruction. I cannot emphasize how deleterious it was for those students taking part-time faculty who knew nothing about the teaching of composition. Since I was able to substitute for quite a few part-time faculty during my tenure at Pikes Peak Community College, I was able to see "behind the curtain" about what other part-time faculty were teaching (or not teaching) in the same course I was teaching. Although the English department gave general parameters about what to teach in any given composition class, it did not mean the new part-time instructor had any knowledge in that area. I went into classrooms as a substitute and asked the students what I could do to help them with their writing. They indicated that the instructor they had did not know what they were doing and that they in turn were unclear about what the writing was supposed to be. They also indicated that the instructor was teaching them "the language of rhetoric" which I found out to be the fallacies in argumentative writing. Students indicated that many of the concepts were explained poorly because they were looking up the concept on their phones at the same time the instructor was teaching it. The instructor did not know what ad hominem, hasty generalization, appeal to authority and red herring meant in the context of writing, because the instructor has no formal education in the teaching of rhetoric.

Perhaps the greatest failure of the teaching of English at the community colleges was the lack of preparation to teach writing. In fact, many English instructors that were hired to teach composition classes were unprepared to do so. Thus, to ensure quality instruction for all of the students who attend the college, it is imperative that part-time faculty be given as much support as possible to guarantee that students are getting good instruction.

Chapter 2:
English Departments Should Know What Writings Four-Year Colleges Assign

The community college writing program in the state of California has established parameters for them by the University of California system of colleges. The writing requirements established by the University of California are designed to ensure that students transferring to their colleges are prepared to do the writing at those colleges. The University of California schools, to ensure that students who are getting a degree are literate, require eleven courses in writing writing from their students. I know. My daughter went to the University of California at Santa Barbara and wrote many papers for her Communications degree. So, community colleges must know what kinds of writing they want their students to see if they transfer to one of the colleges in California. The main paper to learn in the first-year English class is the Modern Language Association research paper.

The MLA paper required for the first-year English class is an argumentative research paper with given parameters. In short, the California colleges want the transferring students to know how to write an MLA-style research paper to perform effectively at the next level. The community colleges do not have to ask these colleges what kinds of papers students need to write because they tell them what is best for their transferring students to be able to write when they get there. In this regard, I found that California was ahead of other states in preparing its students for the four years after coming out of community colleges.

When I was at Pikes Peak Community College, there needed to be more communication between the college and the four-year colleges in the state. The freshman English class did not require writing the MLA-style research paper, something I thought needed to be fixed with their program. In other words, the English department was not looking forward to preparing students for the writing they might do at the four-year colleges. How is it possible for a freshman English class not to write a research paper? That paper aims to prepare students for the inevitable work they will do at four-year colleges in Colorado. When a community college ignores the future writing of its students, they are not looking forward and are not serving its students well. I was troubled by what writings this college was asking students to write. They appeared to be hung up on the idea that students had to write a reflective paper, another brainstorm by some enterprising English teacher who thought this was a great idea.

When I transferred from Fullerton Community College to Cal State University, Fullerton, I was not ready to complete the MLA-style research paper because the English department at the community college did not prepare us for that. We had to learn it independently, and the learning curve was big. English professors at Cal State Fullerton were not sympathetic and graded papers accordingly. I learned quickly to do it right, but the difficulty was more in typing the paper than writing it. Not long after the mid-1960s, colleges were insistent on teaching students to write papers in the first-year English class in preparation for the four year college. There were two semesters of English that students must pass to transfer to Cal State or University of California schools. Learning to write that paper independently took more work than teaching it to the student. I learned by experience instead of by my training in community college.

Students who transfer from community colleges to four-year schools take their knowledge and help students without the necessary background to write papers. It is also essential to determine if there are any assessment tests for students to take in the event of transferring to a four-year college. A look at the assessment test will help guide the teachers as they prepare the students.

Chapter 3:
English Department Should Hire More Composition Instructors

I am sure the readers of this book are tired of the mantra that English teachers are not writing teachers. There are reasons why they are not, a reminder to us that the system needs to change. Again, English instructors hired at the community colleges are literature professors, not composition instructors. Almost all of the full-time faculty and part-time instructors are individuals possessing either a master's degree or a Ph. D in literature. Given that, it does not mean they are capable composition instructors. In fact, most are not. I wish to explain why that is in this chapter.

Most of those hired to teach at the community college are literature teachers, not writing instructors. Many do not know how to teach composition. Teaching composition is an art in itself, just as teaching literature is. Both are separate skills that are learned in separate programs. One can earn a master's degree in literature that sometimes turns into a Phd in literature. English teachers who earn the degrees are prepared to teach literature to students at the community college and the four year college. However, a degree in composition is also a complete master's degree with an entirely different specialization is the teaching of composition. Unfortunately, as has been stated, most of those hired at the community college earned a master's degree in literature. Ironically, most of the courses taught at the community college are composition courses and not literature courses. Why are we hiring literature teachers to teach composition? Although there are literature classes to be taught, the number of them pales by comparison to the composition classes that are to be taught. In short, all of the community colleges at which I taught had numerous literature teachers teaching composition classes. So, the question is, can an instructor with a degree in literature teach composition classes? Yes, but not as well as an instructor with a degree in composition.

When substituting for English teachers at Pikes Peak Community College, I discovered that most of the instructors were not teaching students to exercise the writing process while writing their papers. Instead, most instructors assigned writing. They provided directions about the paper's content requirement and asked that the paper be submitted on a given date. In other words, they were assigning writing and not teaching writing. The instructors should have been using the writing process to teach students that real writers write, get feedback, and rewrite until the paper is as good as one can accomplish in the given period. Then the paper is submitted for evaluation. However, many of those "teaching" compositions were assigning essays like they were assigned essays when they worked for their degree in literature. I found that many community college English teachers did not teach writing as a process. They did not do so because their lack of training in the teaching of writing did not allow them to know better. Perhaps it was because they were not writers themselves, and did not learn the process of writing a paper or a longer work.

While at Pikes Peak Community College, I watched presentations by full-time faculty about how to teach a given writing, and their lack of knowledge about teaching writing was clearly demonstrated. It appeared to me that the concern was more about what the individual instructor wanted to teach than if the required writing was helpful to the student's future writing projects. Many of the writings required were not forward looking to the four year colleges the students would eventually attend. Even though Common Core had become the required educational standard for many states, this community college did not know that the argumentative writings were required at the high school level. In other words, this community college was unaware of the new writing mandates of Common Core. What I saw was an uninformed effort to teach argumentative writing. There was a great deal of focus on covering the fallacies of writing. When I substituted for these instructors, several of these faculty misspoke about them to their students. A good deal of this poor teaching can be attributed to hiring of part-time faculty with degrees in literature and not in composition. When a college has instructors who are not composition instructors but literature instructors, it is no wonder that the teaching of composition was such a failure.

There was additional evidence of a lack of knowledge about teaching composition. I saw very few argumentative papers assigned to students. Instead, the English department had the students writing a rhetorical analysis paper. This is not something one will do for any class other than an English class, and it does not prepare the students for the writings they will do at the four-year colleges. There were additional required assigned papers devised by an English department that demonstrated they knew little about the teaching of composition. They required a synthesis paper, a proposal paper, (which was okay) and a reflective essay. A synthesis paper is not a standard paper written at the four year college. And a reflective paper is something one will do if one is looking at the way in which one composes their writings. One reflects on the writing process, but there was no mention of the writing process in this English department. This was an English department pretending to know how to teach argumentative writing but teaching very few argumentative writings to the students!

Unless one can point to the purpose of these papers, there could have been a better use of time. Although there was one writing that I agreed with, the argumentative essay, there was no argumentative research paper in English 121, the transferable freshman English class. How are students going to be able to do the writings at the four year colleges if they are not taught to do the argumentative research paper? If someone from the full-time faculty can explain how several of these papers have merit at the four-year college or even the community college itself, then I am willing to listen. On the other hand, all of the papers required to be written in the freshman classes at community colleges in California were a direct preparation for the writings the students will do at the four year colleges. The writings that English teachers assign should have merit and usefulness at the next level of learning. I did not see enough evidence of that at Pikes Peak Community College, but most California community colleges freshman English classes were a great preparation for the four year colleges.

Chapter 4:
Community Colleges Need to Significantly Change the Part-Time to Full-Time Ratios

English departments should significantly change the part-time to full-time instructors' rations. The number of part-time faculty substantially impacts the quality of the instruction given to students. Part-time instructors are often less capable than a fully vetted full-time instructor. The community colleges need to increase the number of full-time faculty members.

One of the gravest problems of the community college system is the ratio of full-time to part-time instructors. There should be a 75% to 25% ratio of full-time to part-time teachers, but community colleges do not have that ratio balance. "California's community colleges do not employ enough full-time faculty, and in some cases, districts are misspending state funds allocated for those faculty instead [of hiring] part-time adjuncts," according to a new report from California's state auditor.

Despite a California law that set the goal of a 75 to 25 percent ratio of full-time to part-time teachers, this goal has been largely ignored, and the money allocated for full-time faculty was used for other projects. What this has meant to the instruction of students in the community colleges is that they have been subjected to part-time faculty who may not be as prepared for the teaching at the college. Sometimes, a department head of English is so desperate for part-time faculty that almost anyone who comes close to the credentials is hired. I have seen instructors hired who couldn't find their room. I have seen faculty members say they do not know the subject but will do their best to teach it. Most of the time they are instructors assigned to teach writing courses when their degrees are in the teaching of literature. The quality of instruction is drastically affected by an overabundance of part-time faculty. Community college education can improve greatly with the hiring of more full-time faculty who are qualified to teach at that level of learning.

Although the California legislature has made some efforts to increase the number of full-time to part-time faculty members, the rations still need to be revised. Community colleges continue to use part-time faculty to do most of the teaching, and the students only suffer from this behavior. There is a law, but it has no teeth, and because it is weak, community college districts ignore it. The education of the students suffers as a consequence.

Chapter 5:
Community Colleges Need to Control the Nepotistic and Cronyistic Hiring

When full time positions become available at the community colleges, a better system of hiring these new instructors needs to be employed. Unfortunately, instead of hiring the most qualified instructors, cronyism and nepotism are the methods by which too many instructors are hired. Since department heads and their friends employ most instructors, a more objective hiring process for new faculty positions is necessary. During my many years of teaching at the community colleges, inappropriate hiring was the most significant issue in community colleges. The public is being cheated out of the best candidates when inferior candidates are hired by friends or relatives. To demonstrate the severity of this problem, let me share a couple of stories that will make the reader cringe about cronyistic hiring.

An administrator at one of the community colleges I was associated with managed to get her boyfriend hired to teach at the college. I learned about the hiring of full-time faculty because I drank beer with several full time faculty, and we talked about everything. The boyfriend who was hired was incompetent and needed help putting a lesson plan together. He was not improving students' skills in any of his English classes. Students immediately became aware of his ineptness and dropped out of his class. Sometimes, his classes only had three or four students. Since the discovery of his ineptness took longer than his ability to gain tenure, there wasn't much the administration could do about it. However, the incompetence was so extraordinary, the administration went after him anyway. The leadership was incapable of removing the instructor because of tenure, and it was an ongoing problem for the several years I worked in that district. Their attempt to rid him as a professor was never consummated. In the meantime, students suffered at the hands of this incompetent instructor. I was bothered by the fact that such a poor professor was hired by an administrator friend.

Another hire in one of the community colleges was a crony hire. She was a friend of the department head, and she got a full time job despite the fact she could hardly write her name. The articulation of her sentences was that of a fifth grader. But she got the job because she was a friend of the department chair. She was someone who would not challenge the authority of the department chair, and she was hired partly for that reason. Additionally, this same department head would hire another friend that caused a major stir at the college and eventually got the entire board of education involved with the corruption of hiring at this community college.

If the reader managed to read my first book, then there are plenty of examples of how the public gets less than it should because of these nepotistic and cronyistic hires. The practice is unfair to the public, who deserve the best instructors hired for positions at these public colleges. The school's administration needs to correct this problem. As I indicated in my memoir, one community college took action and established a system to prevent the hiring of friends and relatives. That is the way it should be.

Chapter 6:
Community Colleges Should Establish an Introduction to College Class

The English department can construct and add a new course that reintroduces students to college with a reading, writing, and study skills class. This introductory course will allow students to acclimate themselves to the college learning environment.

An introductory college class is an essential feature of a sound community college. This class will introduce students to the fundamentals of getting a college education. I taught a course like this at Cypress College for five and a half years. It was a great class to teach for students coming to college for the first time or reentering college after a lapsed period. The features of this class included an introduction to reading, writing, and study skills for the college level.

Many reading skills were taught in this course, and having a reading lab faculty make learning much more accomplished. Without enumerating all these skills, the skills taught included how to read a textbook; skimming and scanning skills, rapid reading skills, vocabulary development and comprehension skills.

Aside from reading skills, writing skills were also taught. They included teaching the student how to write excellent introductory, developmental and concluding paragraphs. Students were taught how to draft a thesis, and they learned how to support the thesis. a claim. Aside from these composition skills, students were taught sentence structure, how to vary their sentences, and how to improve their grammar and usage in the context of their writings. Additionally, students were taught the fundamental usage terms in the English language: the difference between "affect" and "effect," " less" and "fewer," and a myriad of other common usage mistakes.

Students were taught essential study skills needed to succeed at the college. Study skills included the ability to manage one's time, read a textbook, read an article, draft a paper, annotating a textbook, and learning how to study materials. Much of the study skills teaching came from a book called *How to Study in College* by Walter Pauk. It was the book I used to prepare myself for college study, and it was very beneficial to the students in my back to college course. One particular part that I emphasized in the reintroduction to college class was time management. We completed a time management sheet for students to follow to assist them in accomplishing their goals for that semester. Many students found that managing their time better enabled them to complete their other courses simultaneously with my introduction to college courses.

Students who take a back-to-college course are more likely to be successful as students than those who do not know how to get organized to complete a college degree. I highly recommend that all community colleges require students to take an introductory to college class when they first begin their college education.

Part B:
Writing Hallmarks
Chapter 7:
Community College English Teachers Should Emphasize Reading and Writing Instead of Grammar

In my first book on teaching English, *Confessions of an English Teacher: A Memoir of My Teaching Years,* I related the story of an articulate and curious second language student at Santa Ana College. She asked why they were studying so much grammar for the course and wondered if this was helping them learn the English language. I had to tell her and the entire class that I did not think it was helping them, but I was mandated to teach it. I told her and the class that the English department makes the decisions about what is to be taught to the students and that part-time faculty have no input about the decisions related to what is to be taught to the students. She then asked what my recommendations would be for them to improve their ability to know English better.

I told them they needed to read and then write about their reading and that they would acquire the English language more rapidly if they did this day after day. I told them they had to read something they could comprehend but something that was also challenging. I told them that the more they read and write about what they read, the more they will advance their English skills more quickly than anything else. Also, I suggested that they take reading courses at the college because they would teach them new vocabulary to improve their language development. She knew instinctively that the study of grammar had no bearing on the improvement of her ability to articulate the language. I encouraged them to read as much as possible because it was the way in which their language would develop more quickly. As the class continued, my interest in teaching them grammar waned. I had students read materials I duplicated, and we wrote about the readings. I demonstrated what I felt they needed to do to advance their language more quickly. They were enormously grateful for my showing them the way to a better understanding of learning the English language. No one cared what I was doing with those students in my classroom anyway. The English department was happy that the course was being taught.

English departments must eliminate the outdated approach of using grammar to teach writing and purportedly improve the language skills of students. The notion that teaching grammar will improve students' writing skills is old-fashioned and naive. English teachers must allow students to read and then write about their reading. Writing is improved with writing rather than through the teaching of excessive grammar. The greatest failure of community colleges is their reliance on teaching grammar as a vehicle for better writing. As I have already indicated in the high school section of this book, grammar stifles writing growth instead of improving it.

During my tenure with each of the community colleges, I learned that the reliance on the teaching of grammar as a so-called method to improving writing was so heavy that it bordered on outright insanity. How did English departments at community colleges get so stuck on teaching grammar as a method to improve writing? I want to provide some history of the problem so that English departments at that level can reevaluate their approach to teaching English.

English teachers were never grammarians. In fact, English majors were not required to take one class in the teaching of grammar. As it has been indicated, they took degrees in literature. In addition to earning a degree in literature, they needed to learn how language is acquired and how to teach writing. I cannot imagine how English departments at community colleges came to the conclusion that students who score poorly on a grammar test cannot write. It appears that when students arrived at the community colleges for instruction in English, the English departments discovered that not all students came to the college with the same language skill levels. So, the brilliant English department determined that they would evaluate their language levels with a grammar test. According to these brilliant English teachers, the grammar test measured how well one can write. The poorer the performance on the grammar test, the stronger the indication to them that the student could not write. So, in their infinite wisdom, they assigned grammar instruction to the student. In other words, the lower the performance on a grammar test, the lower the level of placement in an English course. The student was then forced to take a grammar class that supposedly would improve their writing ability! Does that demonstrate how little English teachers know about the acquisition of language? Ironically, most of them acquired the language they possess through the reading of literature and not through the study of grammar!

When I went to Fullerton Community College as a student, a grammar test was used to place us in the "right" English class. One might end up in the lowest English class if the score on the grammar test were weak. Those students who performed well on the grammar entrance test were placed in the highest level of English. They were likely taught grammar in high school. Those who were not taught grammar in high school performed poorly on the test and were placed in the lowest level English class. Our high school did not teach grammar, and so many of us did not do well on the "English Entrance Exam" (if one wants to call that an entrance exam). Despite the ignorance of that exam, all students were required to take it for placement in an English class. If they did not do well, the "solution" to their problem was to require them to take an English class steeped in grammar. This "solution" to the inability of a student to do well on a grammar test was the remediation of their grammar knowledge. In short, the English teaching tradition decided that teaching a student more grammar will make them better writers. Thus, the tradition of teaching grammar as the solution to poor writing (actually, a poor performance on a grammar entrance exam) was born.

When students arrived in their English classes, they were met with books that included a great many grammar exercises. The lowest level of English was an entire semester of grammar instruction. At one of the colleges, a full time English instructor decided that he would teach only those classes, and he taught seven of them—-five for his full time requirement and two additional classes to earn bonus income. He taught all these grammar classes because it required one book, one lesson plan and scantron tests to grade the student's performances. The additional intent was to avert having to assign any writing in the course because the English department (in their infinite wisdom) required the teaching of grammar to these poorly performing entrance exam students. The course required no writing!

Students were then required to take a second English class that emphasized grammar but also required them to learn writing. The writing required were paragraphs and short essays. Students were being prepared for their final two classes of English, freshman English for two semesters. But the second prerequisite class to freshman English was a whole semester of additional grammar and several short writing assignments. Again, English teachers who designed the course had the view that the more grammar a student is taught, the more it will prepare the students for freshman English. All of this time is wasted if one is expecting to improve the written language of students. If students had spent all of that time reading instead of studying grammar, their language would have improved dramatically. If students had spent all of that time reading and writing, their language skills would have improved dramatically. Instead, an excessive dose of grammar actually drives the writing ability of a student backwards. The linguistic study of a language does not make a student have the ability to use that language more effectively. Reading is the vehicle to improve the use of language. Why wouldn't an English teacher, one who majored in reading literature, not understand that?

It is best to replace all the time spent studying grammar with reading and writing activities. Teaching usage can take place during feedback sessions on the students' writing. Language can only be improved with the combination of reading and writing. The study of grammar should be put to rest and only taught in the context of writing. It is a tradition that must be broken once and for all high school and community college English classes.

Chapter 8:
Community College English Departments Need to Improve the Placement of Students in English Classes

E nglish departments need to improve the assessment of students entering college for their placement in the English curriculum. The proper placement of students in an English class should be the English department's number one priority. However, English departments think that a grammar test is a proper placement tool. It isn't. Writing is the proper placement tool. There are other ways to place students as well. If they have taken the SAT or the ACT then either test can properly place them. However, the most accurate means of placing students is a writing sample.

As it has already been discussed, being placed in an English class with a grammar test when they arrive at the college is wrong. Students who are placed in an English class based on a grammar test are usually misplaced. A grammar test does not accurately place students in the correct English class. What if the high school the student attended did not teach grammar? How does a grammar test measure a student's writing ability anyway? As we know, English teachers have a misguided notion that grammar is linked to writing ability. It isn't, but English teachers have believed that and still believe that for the last seventy-five years. Despite all the research showing no relationship between the learning of grammar and the student's writing ability, community colleges have "stuck to their guns" by forcing students to learn grammar to "improve" their writing skills. The irony is that it does not work, and the two have no relationship. All students who score poorly on a grammar test must take the lowest English class. These classes attempt to improve their writing with megadoses of grammar. It will not make any difference to do so.

A writing sample is the best way to assess a student's placement in English. However, English teachers at the community college do not want to read those writing samples because it takes time, and they do not want to do this task. Instead, they find other ways to place the incoming students, and the grammar test, which is graded by a machine, is quick and easy but not accurate as a placement tool.

An alternative method to assess students is with a reading test since it will reveal their reading level, and better reflect their writing ability. A student's reading levels and writing abilities have a more corresponding relationship. A reading test is a second alternative for proper placement if an English department cannot administer a writing sample to entering students. The reading test is a quick and accurate representation of one's writing skills. Students can be measured more accurately with the Nelson-Denny reading test for placement in English classes. It will also allow community colleges to suggest to students who score poorly to add a reading class to their curriculum. With additional reading, the language of the student will improve instead of the traditional approach of a grammar course.

Once the student has been assigned to an English class, the instructor can ask the student to write an essay and "opt-out" of the class with a good performance if they have not qualified for freshman English. In other words, the student can be placed in a higher-level class with a successful performance on a writing sample in the initial class.

Proper placement of students in a composition class is important to the student. English departments should find an acceptable way to place them properly. It is vital not to punish the student by using a method that does not accurately place them. Assessing students using a grammar test is entirely wrong and does not accurately indicate a student's writing ability.

Part III:
Reading Hallmarks

Chapter 9:
Why Every Community College Needs a Reading Department and Reading Lab

Community colleges need to realize the importance of reading classes and a reading department. A full reading department should exist at every community college. The role of that department will be to improve student's language skills and bring them up to college reading levels so that students can succeed at the community college and beyond. There are several important reasons why they should exist if they don't already.

The decline in literacy will place an ever increasing importance on developing language in the local community and community colleges are best suited to do so. Reading departments should be established on all community college campuses since literacy and students' ability to handle college curricula has significantly diminished. I taught at one community college for over ten years and it was absolutely incredible that it did not have a viable reading department. They did not have one because the English department did not understand the important role that reading improvement has in developing literacy. Instead, the English department thought that language improvement could happen with more grammar instruction. English departments did not have the "mind set" of thinking that a reading department was necessary for language development. They thought the idea was absurd with most of them thinking that reading doesn't need to be taught to college students. Oddly, they felt that language improvement would come from their inundation of students with grammar classes. It was and has been a total failure for seventy-five years!

A reading department and reading classes will put students in the language acquisition mode. That is, language is acquired through the process of reading, not through the process of studying linguistics. The irony of this can be revealed with this simple understanding: English teachers acquired all of their language skills reading literature. They read a great deal of literature and they wrote about that literature. English classes should approach the improvement of a student's language skills with the same understanding. English classes should be about reading and then writing about the reading and language growth will be more assured. Instead of bombarding students with the study of the linguistics of the English language, students who are deficient in their ability to articulate the English language should be reading and writing. For students who are woefully language deficient, they should take reading classes to develop their acquisition of the language through reading and vocabulary development. Therefore, more reading instructors will be needed to handle the load of students needing reading remediation.

When my children grew up, we made sure they were readers. Most importantly, we read to them when they were old enough to sit up. Reading to a child in the first five years of life will set up the child's success. Without reading to the child, the child will lack the vocabulary to keep up with the work in school. Therefore, parents must read to their children as early as possible. Parents might think reading to a one-year-old is ridiculous, but studies have shown that the accumulation of sounds starts as early as when they are born.

As I indicated in the community college section of my memoir, all community colleges need reading classes and a reading lab. For example, instead of a reading program to improve their students' language levels, Santa Ana College had students taking all levels of English courses that taught mounds of grammar. Second language students and native-speaking students who lack reading abilities attended the school only to be required to learn vast amounts of grammar in their English classes. The design of this curriculum is the consequence of English teachers believing grammar instruction "improves" students' language levels. Their choice, of course, was to bombard them with grammar instruction. This action was to the detriment of countless thousands of students whose language never nudged a millimeter forward with excessive grammar instruction. This action also affected English as a Second Language students, who were forced to take many grammar courses to "advance" their skills. Many of these students needed more language improvement and took to cheating with their writing to advance to the next level of learning English. I say this because I had two students in the same class turn in the same word-for-word piece of writing. When I questioned where they got the paper, neither answered me, but it came from a writing group providing the writing for money. Students who finally arrive at the level where writing is measured are not ready to write successfully because they spend excessive hours studying grammar. They resort to cheating on the writing assignments in order to pass the class.

A reading program would advance students' language instead of sending it backward as grammar instruction does. Reading courses will improve the language levels of those students who are deficient in language. The reading classes will teach the students vocabulary and how to read all kinds of literature, including nonfiction and textbooks. The goal is to increase language skills instead of studying linguistics.

The lack of reading labs was the most disheartening aspect of my teaching at community colleges (aside from how people are hired). Reading labs are essential for students to advance their literacy. Reading departments and reading labs are also there to advance the language of students who need to advance it sufficiently in high school (probably because there was no reading program for students there). I was shocked when I arrived at Santa Ana College and found no reading lab. The community has many second-language residents. I wondered how they improved their students' language without providing a reading lab, only to find that the college had grammar instruction to improve their students' language. As we know, grammar does not improve a student's language skills. And who makes the decisions for students' language development? The English department.

Reading courses and labs are placed under the control of the English department, many of whom know nothing about the teaching of reading. Reading departments should be an entity all of itself and not connected to the English department for decision making. Reading labs require the knowledge of a reading specialist with a master's degree or a Phd in reading. English teachers should not make decisions about reading classes or labs. English teachers, ironically, need to learn how language is acquired. Reading labs are designed to diagnose and remediate students' reading issues, and they should be manned by full-time reading instructors with the reading specialist credential and the ability to diagnose reading problems. Reading departments should exist on every community college campus because reading deficiencies will always exist in our communities. A reading lab is a language growth room. In this place, students who diligently work at improving vocabulary and comprehension skills will eventually arrive at college-level reading in a relatively short period versus the false hope that grammar instruction has for students' language growth.

Reading classes are designed to improve students' language levels. Students in a reading class will read, improve their vocabulary, and improve their overall reading skills. Reading is the vehicle for enhanced language development. Reading will improve the grammar of students. Reading will bolster students' vocabulary, and reading will improve students' writing abilities as well. Why have community colleges yet to learn this instead of sticking to the traditional belief that grammar instruction improves students' language levels?

I am sure all those English department college instructors did not become better readers and writers just by studying grammar. Instead, they were readers and writers. Without reading labs to support reading classes, language growth will not improve. Again, reading labs must be instituted at all community colleges to address the ever-increasing literacy decline in American society.

Conclusion

In section one of the book, I illustrate the hallmarks of the great high school English department. English departments that have organized their courses with outlines and lesson plans for those new teachers arriving to teach are well ahead of others who ignore such a feature. English departments that find a way to assess the student's progress in the English program have established a measure of their work that can demonstrate their competence and accountability. I suggested that someone should lead English programs with at least a master's degree and perhaps even a Phd. English departments should be aware of the research on teaching reading, writing, and literature. English departments should choose new teachers from the best candidates and should make their best instructors their mentor teachers.

Outstanding high school English departments have an established writing program. They also offer instruction for teachers who need to be made aware of the teaching of writing. Great English departments teach writing as a process and employ a consistent evaluation program. Good English programs do not waste time learning grammar in isolation of writing and spend a good deal of time teaching usage and grammar in the context of the student's writing. The English department should be aware of the writing local colleges assign so they can prepare their students for that type of writing. English departments teach the literary essay and provide a writing lab for students to complete their papers.

Great English departments that qualify have a Title I reading program and a reading lab to support such a program. They also develop an independent reading program for students to enhance their reading abilities and a context based vocabulary program to build their word skills. English teachers know the world of teaching reading and its impact on students' lives. Finally, great English departments have a well-organized literature program that includes reading nonfiction and literature. Although these hallmarks may cover several aspects of teaching English, English departments need to evaluate whether they possess them.

Community college English departments should establish course outlines and lesson plans for their part-time instructors. English departments should also know what writing their students will do at the four-year colleges they will attend so the community colleges can prepare those students for their eventual writing at that level. Community colleges need to hire more composition instructors. Instructors that are composition teachers are more important than instructors with a literature background. Community colleges must address the full-time to part-time ratios that are out of sync with what is reasonable for all community colleges. Community colleges can improve the performance of new students by offering a reintroduction to college class. Community college English departments need to improve their ability to place students in English classes properly. Finally, community colleges need to establish entire reading departments with reading labs and reading instructors to handle the many students coming to them in the future who need to prepare linguistically to handle the rigors of a college education.

Through my experience teaching at these high schools and community colleges, I have reached these conclusions and recommendations to improve the quality of the English departments at both levels of education. Some of these recommendations will come under fire, but I am certainly willing to listen to other arguments about how English can be better taught at either level of learning.

Works Cited

Chapter 10

Dunn, Patricia A. "Teaching Grammar Improves Writing." *Bad Ideas About Writing*. P. 144.

Chapter 15

Gioia, Dana. *National Endowment for the Arts*. p. 5, 6.

Chapter 16

Rasinski, Timothy. "Webinar: Vocabulary "Practice and Reading Proficiency." <https://www.learninga-z.com/site/resources/breakroom-blog/dr-rasinski-vocabulary-webinar>

Chapter 17

Rasinski, Timothy. "Webinar: Vocabulary "Practice and Reading Proficiency." <https://www.learninga-z.com/site/resources/breakroom-blog/dr-rasinski-vocabulary-webinar>

Chapter 22

Burke, Michael. "California Community Colleges Rely Too Much on Part-time Faculty and Misspend Funds, Audit Finds." February 27, 2023. <(https://edsource.org/2023/california-community-colleges-rely-too-much-on-part-time-faculty-and-misspend-funds-audit-finds/686030)>

Acknowledgments

I want to thank my wife, Tina, for all her love and support while writing this book. She allowed me the space and time to complete something I have always wanted to do: write. I am eternally grateful for her help reading and commenting on the manuscript. She has also helped me grow as a writer by offering insightful comments on my prose. I love you, Tina Kay Sinay.

My heartiest thank you goes to Sue Krenwinkle, an English teacher and friend who offered great insights and suggestions for reworking parts of the book. With her tireless efforts, the book has the quality of presentation it does. It is always best to put the work in the hands of someone who knows what one is talking about, and Sue had many years of teaching experience to validate my claims. Sue presented great ideas that helped shape the book. Thank you.

Author Biography

Richard Sinay was a high school and college English and reading teacher for schools in Orange County, California, for thirty-five years. He spends most of his time playing golf, reading, and writing. He has five publications: *Who We Met on the Way to Stanford: A Father's Memoir,* the story of who he and his son met in the golf world. Fittingly, the book *How to Get a Golf Scholarship to Stanford: A Parent's Guide* is intended for those parents who want to see their golfer play for Stanford. His third publication, *Observations of America and My Ancestral Past: An Epistolary Autobiography,* is a daily account of a twenty-five thousand-mile trip around the country. His subsequent work, *Crazy Little Children Are Jangling the Keys of the Kingdom: The Estrangement Epidemic in America,* examines the estrangement epidemic in America. Following that, his *Confessions of an English Teacher: A Memoir of My Teaching Years* is the first book about teaching English in California high schools and community colleges. His latest publication, Confessions of an English Teacher: How English Departments in High School and Community Colleges Can Improve Instruction, follows his memoir. He resides in Palm Desert, California, with his wife, Tina.

www.ingramcontent.com/pod-product-compliance
Lightning Source LLC
Chambersburg PA
CBHW071155120626
46546CB00006B/2270